WELSH
COUNTRY RECIPES

COMPILED BY
SARAH & ANN GOMAR

RAVETTE BOOKS

Published by Ravette Books Limited
3 Glenside Estate, Star Road
West Partridge Green, Horsham,
Sussex RH13 8RA
(0403) 710392

Production: Oval Projects Ltd.
Cover design: Jim Wire
Typesetting: Artset Graphics
Printing & binding: Norhaven AS

All recipes are given in Imperial and Metric
weights and measures. Where measurements
are given in 'cups', these are American cups,
holding 8 fluid ounces.

The recipes contained in this book are traditional
and many have been compiled from archival sources.
Every effort has been made to ensure that the recipes
are correct.

The wooden Loving Spoon on the front cover is part
of the collection of handmade Welsh crafts available
from Bwrdd Croeso Cymru (Wales Tourist Board)
34 Piccadilly, London W1, whose kindness is
gratefully acknowledged.

RECITES

VEGETABLE DISHES

CHEESE DISHES

BAKESTONE COOKERY - BREAD and SCONES

PRESERVES

DRINKS

SWEETS

SUNDRIES

WALES

Wales is a very beautiful country with greatly contrasting scenery - mountains, rolling hills, rivers, lakes and a long coastline, all of which have shaped the national diet.

Wales is famous for excellent mutton and lamb. The native breed is the small, hardy, Welsh Mountain Sheep which produces soft high quality wool as well as sweet, tender meat. Lamb is an ingredient of many well known Welsh recipes, including cawl and pies. Shepherds were accustomed to curing salt hams (lamb) at home. Legs of lamb were laid in a mixture of salt, or saltpetre, treacle and spices for three weeks before being smoked in sawdust over a fire of peat, beech and turves.

From the 16th century until the growth of the railways around 1850, cattle, sheep and pigs were driven from Wales to St. Bartholomew's Fair in London and other big cities. It is estimated that in the mid-18th century, fifteen thousand cattle, five thousand pigs and many thousands of sheep made the great trek to England every year from Anglesey alone. The sheep and cattle swam the Menai Straits, but pigs were brought over in boats to avoid cutting their throats with their trotters. Geese were also driven to market and were "shod" for the long journey by dipping their feet in pitch and fine sand.

Today many Inns on the old drovers' routes have names like the 'Drovers Arms', 'Drovers Roads', 'Welsh Ways', and 'Welsh Runs', and a Drover's pie is still made and sold locally of minced lamb and onions topped with mashed potato in a pastry case.

Wales has a plentiful supply of excellent fish as well as an important fishing industry. River trout, sea trout known as sewin, salmon, mackerel and herring have long been served on the table in many delicious ways. Shellfish too have been a source of income and nutrition. Cockles were gathered from the sands at low tide and taken in wooden carts drawn by donkeys and ponies from the beach to be sold in the markets of Swansea and Cardiff. Oyster and mussel beds along the Menai Straits have been revived and lobsters, scallops, crabs, shrimps and all kinds of shellfish are much enjoyed.

Another delicacy is an edible seaweed called laver. It is gathered from the rocks in South Wales and used to be cured in long drying houses on the beach. It is popular covered with oatmeal and fried with bacon for breakfast or made into a sauce to accompany fish and meat. Sampkin, another edible seaweed is gathered from the rocks in spring, boiled, and eaten dipped in vinegar.

Wales is also famous for its dairy produce, creamy milk, butter and cheese produced from the herds of dairy and beef cattle kept in the lowlands and rolling hills. The Welsh have always loved cheese especially toasted cheese (caws pobi) — thickly sliced and toasted in front of the fire, the forerunner of Welsh rarebit. Cheese was not only an everyday food, it was eaten at celebration meals such as Christmas and harvest time. Wales produces a variety of good farmhouse cheeses from cheddar to goats milk.

Its most famous cheese, Caerphilly or Caws caerffili, is a light, crumbly, easily-digested cheese which originates from the Mid-Glamorgan town of that name. It was popular with the miners, as it was convenient to take down the pit, and it was said did not repeat when bending down.

Hard conditions have given rise to many traditional dishes, particularly cawl - the complete meal of meat and vegetables made with whatever ingredients are available. When times were hard, cawl was popular and economic. Cooked in one pot over the fire it provided two family meals. First the meat was eaten with the potatoes. Next day the vegetables were served in the left-over broth aptly called Cawl Twymo or second cawl. In some areas cawl made in a kettle with a short wide spout and a lid which enabled the broth to be poured off and the meat and vegetables to be left behind. It is traditionally served in wooden bowls and eaten with special hand-carved wooden spoons, which varied from region to region, or in attractive pottery bowls decorated with flowers.

The staple food of the people apart from cawl was oats, reaped with the sickle. Oats are very nutritious. They are high in fat and protein and the Welsh have many ways of cooking and eating them such as Llymru, an oatmeal cereal eaten with treacle or honey; Uwd, a set porridge made from oatmeal juices (a large quantity of which would be taken to the fields during harvest time to eat with milk or beer and bread and butter); Griwel blawd ceirch, a gruel made from steeping oatmeal in water and milk; and Bwdram, a flummery eaten with herrings at suppertime which was considered to be particularly nutritious for nursing mothers.

In the mid-18th century a typical day's meals for everyone who came to help a farmer with the harvest was breakfast of bread, cheese and milk, a huge midday meal of Llymru with bread and butter, and supper of cawl made of beef and mutton with vegetables and a pudding, all washed down with quantities of beer and ales.

Traditions involving food are strong in Wales during Christmas and the New Year. Celebration used to begin in many Welsh homes on Christmas Eve with festivities, which included eating and drinking, and continued all night until everybody went to a very early morning religious service known as Plygain. After the church service there was more feasting on hot ale, bread, cheeses and cakes.

An old Christmas custom particularly on Twelfth Night was Wassailing. The Wassail was a large decorative bowl filled with cakes and baked apples and covered with warm ale, which could be taken from one house to another.

Callennig was a New Year tradition in Glamorgan, Carmarthen and Monmouthshire. Young boys carrying fruit, such as oranges on a skewer decorated with holly, mistletoe, raisins and corn, would collect New Year's gifts of cakes or coins, and sing carols.

The custom of holding Noson Lawen — a cheerful evening — dates back to the 17th century in rural Wales. During winter or at harvest time, gatherings were held in farm kitchens and barns. Plenty of good food was available as well as poetry, song and dance and the telling of folk and ghost stories.

Another Welsh tradition was to take currant loaves as wedding gifts to the bride's house the day before the ceremony. The loaves were sliced and sold at suppertime to men who gave them to the young ladies they admired. The girl with the most slices of currant loaf was likely to be the next bride.

Wales is a land of legend, music and song with a language of its own. It is a country not to be missed by the visitor, who is assured of good wholesome food from excellent local produce, and a warm Welsh welcome 'Croeso Cymreig'.

OYSTER SOUP FROM GOWER —
Pastai Bro Gŵyr
Serves 4

During Victorian times there was a very busy and successful oyster fishing industry around the Oystermouth area of the South Wales coast, in the Gower to the west of Swansea. In those days it was common to use 6 dozen or 72 oysters to 8 pints of broth.

2 pints (1.15 litres/4 cups) mutton broth, well skimmed
1 oz (25 g) butter or margarine
2 oz (50 g) flour
2 medium onions
A pinch of mace
Salt and black pepper
12 oysters or more if available
2 tablespoons cream

Skim off any fat from the mutton broth.

Peel and chop the onions.

Melt the fat in a saucepan.

Stir in the flour and cook gently, stirring continuously, for a few minutes.

Gradually add the mutton broth, with the onion, seasoning and mace, still stirring.

Bring to the boil, then simmer for about 30 minutes until the onion is cooked.

Scrub the oyster shells, open and beard the oysters by cutting off the dark fringe round the edges.

Loosen from the shell, and take off the top shell.

Put the oysters into a tureen or individual soup bowls.

Pour the mutton broth over them and swirl in the cream just before serving.

CURRANT DUMPLINGS FOR CAWL

Makes 8 dumplings

Current dumplings are popular served with any soup and can be dropped in and simmered about 45 minutes before the end of cooking time.

4 oz (100 g) fine oatmeal
1 oz (25 g) self-raising flour
1 oz (25 g) shredded suet
Salt and pepper
2 oz (50 g) currants
Cold water to mix

Mix the oatmeal, flour and suet together.

Season with a little salt and pepper.

Stir in the currants.

Mix to a stiff dough with a little cold water.

Knead gently on a floured board.

Shape into dumplings.

Drop into the soup, and simmer for about 45 minutes until light and fluffy

BACON BROTH — Cawl Cig-Moch   Serves 4

A hock end of bacon is the ideal cut for this delicious cawl. The exact amount of meat and vegetables is not important. As a rough idea use about 3 oz (75 g) or one of each type of vegetable used and 8 oz (225 g) of potatoes.

About 1 lb (450 g) mixed bacon and beef, preferably brisket
2 pints (1.15 litres/4 cups) water or stock
Vegetables as available — carrots, leeks, parsnips, potatoes, onion, turnip, swedes and cabbage
A little butter
Salt and pepper
A little oatmeal (optional)
Chopped parsley

Cut up the meat, and peel and chop the vegetables.

Melt the butter in a large saucepan and put in the meat and vegetables, except for the potatoes and leeks if used.

Put on the lid and cook the mixture gently for 5 minutes.

Pour on the water or stock, and season with pepper and salt if required.

Bring to the boil and simmer for 2-3 hours.

Add the potatoes for 30 minutes and the leeks 10 minutes before the end of cooking time.

Mix the oatmeal to a paste with a little water, and stir it into the cawl.

Boil until thickened.

Sprinkle with chopped parsley before serving.

FISH SOUP

This substantial soup can be made from whatever fish is available, and can be as simple or extravagant as wished. It is traditionally made with mussels, winkles and cockles round the Mumbles Coast of South Wales. Shellfish such as shrimps, lobster or crab, or white fish such as cod or haddock can also be used.

1½ lbs (675g) shrimps, mussels, cockles, winkles, lobster
  or crab, cod or haddock
2 carrots
2 medium onions
A small green pepper
1½ lb (675 g) potatoes
2 leeks
6 oz (175 g) streaky bacon
About 1½ pints (900 ml/3¾ cups) milk
A bay leaf
Chopped garlic to taste (optional)
1 wineglassful of dry white wine
Cornflour for thickening
A little butter
Salt and black pepper
Chopped parsley to decorate

Prepare the fish or shellfish according to type, and if appropriate cut into small pieces.

Wash and chop the leeks.

Peel and chop the carrots, onions, pepper and potatoes.

Cut the bacon into small pieces and fry gently in a frying pan until the fat runs.

Add the onions and potatoes and let them soften.

Put the fish into a saucepan and cover with the milk.

Add the vegetables, bacon, bay leaf, garlic, white wine and seasoning.

Cook the soup gently until the fish and vegetables are cooked.

Thicken with a little cornflour mixed with a little butter, adding more milk if required.

Remove the bay leaf and sprinkle with chopped parsley before serving.

LAVERBREAD — Bara Lawr   Serves 4

Laver is a fine dark green seaweed, rich in minerals, which is gathered from the rocks in South Wales, particularly in the Swansea and Pembrokeshire coastal regions. Traditionally it was dried in long, low thatched drying sheds on the beach, and sold from wooden tubs lined with white cloths. It can be bought ready prepared from local markets, butchers, fish and grocery shops and is also available in tins. It is made into cakes with oatmeal to fry and eat with bacon or ham; or used to make a delicious sauce to serve with lamb or shellfish; or spread on toast as a savoury. To prepare the laverbread the seaweed is thoroughly washed to remove all the sand. Then it is boiled for several hours until soft and drained.

For breakfast:
1lb (450 g) purchased ready-prepared laver
2 oz (50 g) oatmeal
Bacon fat for frying
4 rashers Welsh bacon
4 eggs

Mix the laver with the oatmeal and shape into four cakes.

Fry in hot bacon fat for about 5 minutes, and serve with the fried bacon and eggs.

CURRIED EGGS

Serves 4

Spicy curry sauce is also excellent served with chicken, fish or prawns.

2 onions
1 oz (25 g) butter
1 dessertspoonful of curry powder
¾ oz (20 g) flour
½ pint (300 ml/1¼ cups) stock
Salt and pepper to taste
2½ fl oz (4 tablespoons/⅓ cup) cream
4 hard-boiled eggs

To make the curry sauce:

Peel and chop the onion very finely.

Fry in the butter for about 5 minutes until golden brown.

Stir in the flour and curry powder.

Gradually add the stock.

Stir the mixture over the heat until boiling.

Simmer gently for 30 minutes.

Season to taste with the salt and pepper.

Add the cream just before serving and do not allow the sauce to boil again.

To make the curried eggs:

Cut the hard-boiled eggs in half and arrange them on a serving plate.

Pour the curry sauce over the eggs.

Serve hot or cold.

PORT AND STILTON PATÉ

Serves 8

A speciality from the Beaufort Hotel, Tintern.

8 oz (225 g) stilton cheese
2 measures of ruby port
1 medium sized onion
½ lb (225 g) butter
4 oz (100 g) hazel nuts
1 oz (25 g) parsley
1 oz (25 g) paprika
2 tablespoons of double cream
2 drops of anchovy essence

Chop the onion and stilton finely.

Chop the nuts and parsley.

Cream with the butter until the mixture becomes white.

Mix in the port, paprika, double cream, and anchovy essence.

Blend for 1 minute.

Using greaseproof paper roll into the desired shape.

SHRIMP AND CHEESE SAVOURY

Serves 4

After shrimping, shrimps used to be boiled and served with cheese sauce for tea. Shrimps were also made into paste with anchovies and served on toast; or potted with plenty of Welsh butter. This tasty savoury can also be made with prawns.

½ lb (225 g) of cooked shrimps
1 oz (25 g) butter
1 oz (25 g) flour
½ pint (300 ml/1¼ cups) milk
A pinch of salt
1 egg
2 oz (50 g) grated cheese
4 slices of bread, toasted on one side

Shell the shrimps.

Melt the butter in a saucepan over a gentle heat.

Stir in the flour with a wooden spoon and cook for a few minutes.

Gradually add the milk stirring all the time until the mixture is smooth.

Add a pinch of salt and stir in the grated cheese and the shrimps.

Spread the fish mixture over the untoasted side of the bread and brown under the grill for a few minutes.

CHEESY SCALLOPS

Serves 4

4 scallops
½ lb (225 g) mashed potatoes
1 oz (25 g) butter
1 oz (25 g) flour
2 oz (50 g) grated cheese
4 slices of bacon, cooked and diced
¼ pint (150 ml/⅔ cup) milk
¼ pint (150 ml/⅔ cup) cooking stock
2 tablespoons chopped parsley

Cut open the scallop shells (they may be put into a warm oven until the shell opens).

Remove the black sac and any gristly fibre.

Boil the scallops in a pan of salted water for about 10 minutes.

Drain and reserve the stock.

Remove the scallops and clean the shells.

Melt the butter in a pan and stir in the flour.

Cook for a few minutes over a low heat.

Gradually add the milk and stock, stirring until the sauce is smooth and thickened.

Season with salt and pepper.

Stir in the grated cheese and the cooked diced bacon.

Pipe the mashed potato around each shell.

Place a scallop in the middle.

Pour over the cheese sauce and sprinkle with chopped parsley.

TROUT WITH BACON —
Brithyll â Chig Moch

Serves 4

River trout and sewin, sea trout (which is like salmon), were abundant in Wales. The brown river trout is now farmed as it has become very scarce. Trout was cooked in many ways, sometimes simply rolled in seasoned oatmeal, dotted with fat and baked.

This traditional dish was most often served for breakfast but it also makes an excellent supper dish.

4 fresh trout
8 rashers of thin, streaky bacon
Salt and pepper
1 tablespoon freshly chopped parsley

Split and clean the trout.

Remove the bones.

Trim the rind from the bacon and wrap 2 slices around each fish.

Place the trout in a greased, shallow ovenproof dish.

Pack the fish tightly into the dish.

Season with salt and pepper and sprinkle with chopped parsley.

Cover and bake in a hot oven for about 20 minutes but do not overcook the fish.

Oven: 400°F/200°C   Gas Mark 6

BAKED TROUT WITH OATCAKES
AND HONEY
Serves 1

The Beaufort Hotel nestles in the beautiful wooded Wye Valley. It overlooks the magnificent ruins of historic Tintern Abbey, founded in 1131. The Hotel has itself grown up with the history of the Wye Valley. Formerly the Beaufort Arms, many visitors during the early 19th century came by pleasure barge or carriage excursion. A local historian of the time, Mr. Charles Heath wrote: "The larder at the Inn is at all times well supplied."

The Beaufort Hotel has maintained its reputation for good food. Salmon and trout from the river are a speciality of its excellent restaurant, which specialises in local dishes and produce. Baked trout with oatcakes and honey is a favourite.

12 oz (350 g) brown trout, gutted
2 eggs
2 oz (50 g) butter
8 oz (225 g) oats
4 oz (100 g) honey
2 oz (50 g) self-raising flour
Salt and pepper

To cook the trout:

Brush the trout with some of the honey, then roll in approximately 2 oz (50 g) of the oats.

Bake the trout in a medium oven until cooked.

To make the oatcakes:

Mix all the ingredients together. If the mixture is too thick, add a little milk.

Fry on a hot griddle or in a frying pan, until golden brown.

Brush the trout with a little more honey before serving with the oatcakes.

Oven: 350°F/180°C   Gas Mark 4

POACHED SALMON STEAK WITH PRAWN, MUSHROOM AND CUCUMBER SAUCE

FROM THE GEORGE III HOTEL Serves 2

The George III Hotel, situated at the head of the spectacular Mawddach Estuary in the hamlet of Penmaenpool, is well known for good food using local produce. Over 300 years old, it was once two separate buildings - a pub and a ship chandlers, serving a flourishing boat building industry on the river. Chef, David Collett, prepares this dish from fresh local salmon.

2 salmon steaks
½ pint (300 ml/1 ¼ cups) fish stock
¼ pint (150 ml/⅔ cup) dry white wine
2 shallots, finely chopped

To make the sauce:

1 teaspoon fresh tarragon, chopped
1 teaspoon fresh parsley, chopped
3 fl oz (4 ½ tablespoons) double cream
1 oz (25 g) cucumber, peeled, deseeded and chopped
1 oz (25 g) peeled prawns
1 oz button mushrooms
1 tablespoon cornflour
Salt and pepper
2 slices of lemon to garnish

To cook the salmon:

Place the salmon steaks in a poaching tray and cover with the fish stock, white wine, shallots and tarragon.

Simmer gently for about 10 minutes, or until the centre bone is easily removed.

Take the salmon steaks out of the poaching tray, reserving the cooking liquid of the sauce, skin them and keep warm.

To make the sauce:

Strain the cooking liquid and add the rest of the ingreddients, saving a few prawns and some chopped parsley for garnish.

Bring the liquid almost to boiling point and being careful not to over-thicken, add the cornflour and simmer for a further 2 minutes.

To serve:

Place the salmon steaks on a serving dish, cover with the sauce and garnish with the prawns, parsley and lemon slices.

WELSH SALMON

A coracle was used for salmon fishing. The boat was light enough for the fishermen to carry on their backs when ashore. The men would fish in pairs bringing up their net full of salmon stretched between two coracles.

1 salmon
1 oz (25 g) melted butter
A little lemon juice
1 tablespoon finely chopped parsley

Wash the fish and place it whole in salted warm water. (Warm water rather than cold will preserve the colour of the fish.)

Bring to the boil and simmer gently until the fish is tender.

Place the salmon on a hot serving dish, pour over the melted butter and lemon juice and sprinkle with chopped parsley.

Serve hot or cold.

FISH CAKES — Teisennau Pysgod

½ lb (225 g) cooked white fish
2 oz (50 g) breadcrumbs
4 oz (100 g) mashed potatoes
A teaspoon of chopped parsley
1 egg beaten
A teaspoon of salt
A teaspoon of pepper
2 oz (50 g) breadcrumbs
A beaten egg for coating
Lard for frying

Remove any skin and bones and cut up the fish.

Mix the breadcrumbs, potatoes, parsley, egg and seasoning with the fish.

Form the mixture into round cakes of the same size.

Brush each round with a little beaten egg and cover it with
breadcrumbs.

Cook in the hot fat until each side is browned.

MACKEREL WITH FENNEL SAUCE

Serves 4

4 mackerel
2 oz (50 g) butter
1 tablespoon freshly chopped fennel

For the sauce:
2 tablespoons chopped fennel
4 oz (100 g) butter
½ teaspoon pepper
½ teaspoon nutmeg
½ oz (15 g) flour
¼ pint (150 ml/⅔ cup) water

Clean the mackerel thoroughly.

Dot each fish with butter, sprinkle with fennel and season with salt and pepper.

Grill the fish until they are brown on each side.

To make the sauce:

Melt 1 oz (25 g) of the butter in a pan with a little pepper and nutmeg.

Add the flour and cook for a few minutes, stirring with a wooden spoon.

Gradually add the cold water and continue stirring until it boils.

Simmer for 20 minutes.

Gradually whisk in the remaining butter, a teaspoon at a time. This should be done over a gentle heat or in a double saucepan.

Blanch and purée the fennel and stir it into the sauce.

FILLET OF ARCTIC CHAR

Seiont Manor Hotel owned by John and Pippa Evans is a luxurious hotel set in private parkland at Llanrug near Caernarfon. Built around an original Georgian farmhouse it has spectacular views from every window to the sea or to the mountains of Snowdonia. Chef, Richard Treble specialises in haute cuisine as well as local dishes using local produce. This recipe uses the rather rare Arctic Char from nearby Llanberis Lake, but is equally as good made with rainbow trout.

4 char or rainbow trout each weighing about 12 oz (350 g) skinned and filleted
Salt and pepper

For the sauce:
4 shallots, thinly sliced
½ oz (15 g) unsalted butter
7 fl oz (200 ml/¾ cup) dry white wine
2 oz (50 g) field mushrooms, sliced
¼ pint (150 ml/⅔ cup) double cream
A knob of cold, unsalted butter

For the mushroom duxelle stuffing:
4 shallots, finely chopped
1 oz (25 g) unsalted butter
4 oz (100 g) shiitake or oyster mushrooms (or a mixture), chopped
2 oz (50 g) breadcrumbs
1 oz (25 g) unsalted butter
Extra mushrooms for garnish (optional)

To make the sauce:

Season the fish fillets with the salt and pepper.

Set aside while preparing the sauce and mushroom duxelle.

Gently cook the shallots in the butter in a heavy based pan for 5 minutes, or until softened but not coloured.

Deglaze the pan with the wine, stirring well to dissolve any sediment.

Add the mushrooms and simmer for 10 minutes or until the liquid has reduced by half.

Add the cream, bring to the boil, simmer for a minute then pass through a fine sieve, pressing the shallots and mushrooms with a wooden spoon to extract all the juices.

To make the stuffing:

Gently cook the shallots in the butter for 5 minutes until softened, then add the mushrooms and cook for a further 5 minutes.

Add the breadcrumbs and plenty of salt and pepper to taste.

To serve:

When ready to serve, shallow fry the fish fillets in a large frying pan in the remaining butter for 2 to 3 minutes on each side.

Meanwhile reheat the mushroom duxelle and the sauce, and whisk in a knob of chilled butter.

Adjust the seasoning if necessary.

Place a fillet on a warmed serving plate, top with some of the duxelle mixture, sandwich with another fillet.

Continue with the other fillets, spoon the sauce around the fish and serve at once.

If you wish, garnish with sautéed oyster or shiitake mushrooms.

COCKLE AND LAVERBREAD PANCAKES

Serves 4

FROM THE WHITE HORSE INN, LLANDEILO, DYFED

Owners Steve and Marion Williams specialise in Welsh recipes using local produce. Allow 2 pancakes for each person.

For the batter:
4 oz (100 g) flour
A pinch of salt
1 egg
¼ pint (150 ml/⅔ cup) milk

For the cheese sauce:
½ oz (15 g) butter
Cornflour to thicken
½ pint (300 ml/1 ¼ cups) milk
4 oz (100 g) cheese, grated

For the pancake filling:
8 oz (225 g) laverbread
1 lb (450 g) cooked, shelled cockles
Black pepper, freshly ground

To make the cheese sauce:

Melt the butter and stir in the cornflour.

Slowly add the milk, stirring until thick.

Add the grated cheese, and heat gently until melted.

Reserve the sauce for use later.

To make the pancakes:

Make in the normal way (see Welsh Crempog).

The quantity of batter should produce 8 pancakes.

To fill the pancakes:

Spread each pancake with a layer of laverbread (which may be heated beforehand if wished).

18

Add a filling of cockles (which may also be heated beforehand), and sprinkle with fresh black pepper.

Roll up the pancakes.

Cover them with the cheese sauce and place under a hot grill until well browned.

Serve with mixed salad.

PICKLED HERRINGS
Serves 3

This dish is delicious served cold with new potatoes.
6 small herrings
1 teaspoon pickling spice
Salt and pepper
1 large onion, peeled and sliced
2 bay leaves
6 fl oz (175 ml/¾ cup) vinegar
6 tablespoons of water

Remove the heads, clean and fillet the herrings.

Put the fish in an ovenproof dish and season well with salt and pepper.

Put a layer of sliced onion on top of the fish.

Add the spice and bay leaves.

Pour over the vinegar and the water.

Cover the dish and bake in a moderate oven for about an hour or until the herrings are browned and the onions are cooked.

Oven: 350°F/180°C   Gas Mark 4

COCKLE PIE — Pastai Cocos

Serves 4

In South West Wales cockles were gathered by cockle women on the sands. The woman would use a handrake and scraper to collect the cockles, in large wicker baskets, which were then sold in the markets. Cockles were made into soups, pies, cakes or just boiled, shelled and eaten with vinegar and lemon.

½ lb (225 g) shortcrust pastry
2 pints cockles
½ pint (300 ml/1¼ cups) cockle stock
1 bunch of spring onions, chopped
4 slices of bacon, diced
Pepper

Scrub the shells making sure any sand is removed.

Put the cockles into a pan of salted water and boil them for about 2 hours or until the shells open.

Drain and reserve the stock.

Allow the cockles to cool a little then remove the cockles from the shells.

Thickly roll out the pastry on a floured surface and set aside a few strips for decoration.

Line an ovenproof pie dish with the pastry.

Cover the bottom of the pie with the cockles, a layer of onion and finally a layer of bacon, seasoning each layer with pepper.

Pour over the stock.

Lay strips of pastry across the pie to make a lattice pattern.

Bake for about 30-40 minutes in a hot oven or until the pastry is golden brown.

Serve hot with new potatoes or cold with salad.

Oven: 400°F/200°C   Gas Mark 6

CHICKEN CASSEROLE IN WHITE WINE

Serves 4

4 chicken portions
Seasoned flour
8 oz (225 g) bacon
1 onion
2 leeks
½ pint (300 ml/1¼ cups) chicken stock
1 wineglass of dry white wine
Salt and pepper
A little cornflour
Oil for frying

Roll the chicken portions in the seasoned flour.

Heat the oil in a frying pan and fry the chicken to seal on all sides.

Put the chicken in an ovenproof casserole dish.

Remove the rinds and dice the bacon.

Peel and chop the onions.

Lightly fry the bacon and onions.

Wash and chop the leeks and add to the casserole with the bacon and onions.

Pour over the chicken stock mixed with the wine.

Season with salt and pepper if required.

Bake in a moderate oven for about 1 hour.

Thicken with a little cornflour mixed to a smooth cream with water just before serving.

Oven: 350°F/180°C   Gas Mark 4

PHEASANT CASSEROLE

Serves 2-3

1 prepared pheasant
Seasoned flour
Oil for frying
4 rashers of Welsh bacon
1 onion
1 carrot
1 shallot
1 leek
4 oz (100 g) mushrooms
Stock to cover
2 tablespoons of port or sherry (optional)
Salt and pepper

Joint the bird, and roll in the seasoned flour to coat.

Fry the joints in a frying pan until golden brown to seal.

Take the rinds off the bacon, and cut into small pieces.

Peel and slice the onion, carrot and shallot.

Wash and slice the leek and mushrooms.

Put the pheasant joints in the casserole, with the bacon and vegetables.

Pour on sufficient stock just to cover the joints, and add the port or sherry.

Season to taste with salt and pepper.

Cover the casserole dish with a lid or foil, and cook in a moderate oven for about 1 hour, or until tender.

Oven: 350°F/180°C   Gas Mark 4

WELSH SALT DUCK —
Hwyaden hallt Gymreig

Serves 4

This unusual and delicious Welsh method of cooking and serving duck
is not found anywhere else in the country. Welsh cooks recommend
using a large fat duck for the best results. The dish takes three days to
prepare before cooking. The first known recipe comes from Lady
Llanover's book *The first principles of Good Cookery*, which was published in 1867.

1 duck
6 oz (175 g) sea salt
Stock made from the giblets
½ pint (300 ml/1 ¼ cups) for each 1 lb (450 g) of duck
Pepper

Rub the sea salt all over the prepared duck, inside and
out.

Put the bird into a bowl, and leave it in a cool place,
covered with a cloth.

Turn the duck over twice a day for three days, rubbing in
the salt that comes from it again.

After 3 days, rinse well.

Put the duck into a deep close fitting casserole and just
cover it with the stock.

Stand the casserole in a pan of simmering water on top of
the stove for 2 hours, or cook in a moderate oven for 2
hours.

Serve hot with Onion Sauce (see recipe) or cold.

Oven: 325°F/160°C   Gas Mark 3

STUFFED ROAST GOOSE WITH APPLE SAUCE

For the stuffed roast goose:
1 goose
6 large onions
2 oz (50 g) butter
2 tablespoonful powdered sage
2 tablespoonful breadcrumbs
Salt and pepper
Fat for basting
Stock for gravy

For the apple sauce:
2 lbs (900 g) apples
A little sugar
Water

To roast and stuff the goose:

Prepare the goose and wipe it inside with a damp cloth.

Peel the onions, boil them until soft, and chop finely.

Put them in a bowl with the powdered sage, breadcrumbs, salt and pepper.

Mix all well together.

Divide the butter into small pieces and add to the other ingredients.

Stuff the goose with this mixture and truss it for roasting.

Sprinkle the bird with salt, prick the breast and brush lightly with fat.

Put it in a roasting tin and cook in a moderately hot oven for about 1½ hours.

To make the apple sauce:

Peel the apples, cut into quarters, and take out the core.

24

Slice the apples, not too thin and put them into a stewpan with a little sugar and water

Cook them gently until they become a pulp.

Oven: 375°F/190°C   Gas Mark 5

For a Hung Goose

In the National Library of Wales among Eliza Sloughter's beautifully handwritten 18th century recipes and remedies which include the Red Water that Cureth all Green Wounds, burns, old sores and cankers; snaile water for a Consumption or Cough; to pickle sparlings (fish); Lady Elizabeth Edgerton's recipe for the Worms; and Thieves Vinegar to prevent infection, is ...

For a Hung Goose

'Take the largest and fattest Goose you can buy draw it and singe it take ½ an ounce of white salt peter ½ a pound of course sugar mix them with Bay and white salt as much as you think will season it warm your seasoning in an oven or before the ffire and rubb it very well into your Goose, let it lye in the Pickle a ffortnight keep rubbing it every Day then take it out dry and throw it over with Brann then paper and hang it up not too near the ffire and it will be fit to boil in a fortnight or less.'

RABBIT PIE

Serves 4-6

1 rabbit, jointed and chopped
1 leek
A pinch of dried herbs
4 rashers of Welsh bacon, chopped
2 potatoes
Salt and pepper
Some water or stock
8 oz (225 g) shortcrust pastry

Soak the rabbit overnight in salted water.

Rinse and put into a casserole dish.

Peel and slice the leek and potatoes.

Cover the rabbit with the vegetables and bacon.

Season with salt and pepper and sprinkle with herbs.

Add the water or stock to come half way up the dish.

Cover with the pastry, making a hole in the centre for the steam to escape.

Bake in a hot oven for 20 minutes then for 1 hour at the reduced temperature.

Oven: 425°F/220°C   Gas Mark 7
Reduce to: 325° F/160° C   Gas Mark 3

RABBIT STEW

Serves 4

A favourite recipe handed down from mother to daughter in Rhyl, Clwyd.

1 rabbit, cleaned out well and chopped into pieces
2 onions
Dried sage and onion
Mushrooms
Potatoes
Salt and pepper
Water or stock to cover

Soak the rabbit overnight in salted water.

Rinse and put into a casserole dish.

Peel and slice the onions.

Add a good layer of onions to the meat and season with salt and pepper.

Sprinkle with some dried sage and onion and the sliced mushrooms.

Peel and slice the potatoes and add a good layer.

Put in some water or stock to cover.

Cook for about 1 hour in a moderate oven.

Check the seasoning and add more stock if necessary.

Oven: 350°F/180°C   Gas Mark 4

GAME PIE

This recipe is at least 150 years old. It has been handed down through the generations from a farmer's wife in Ruabon. Diners were instructed to: "Clear your plates and kiss the cook"!

It is reported that Sir Winston Churchill on eating this Game Pie asked for the recipe. The cook's reply was: "Then you would be as wise as me, and that would never do!"

For the pie filling:
1 ½ lbs (675 g) venison
2 hind quarters of rabbit or hare
2 pigeons
4 breasts of crow
Bouquet garni, tied in muslin
Freshly milled black pepper
Salt to taste
1 small onion, finely chopped
1 small whole carrot
Sufficient dry red wine to cover

For the gelatine:
3 pigs feet
Water to cover
Salt and pepper

For the pastry:
3 lbs (1.5 kg) plain flour
1 lb (450 g) of best lard
Salt to taste
Beaten egg for wash

Place the ingredients in an earthenware stew jar.

Cover with a lid and simmer until the flesh is tender and drops off the bones.

Strain through a large colander.

Remove the bag of herbs, carrot, and all the bones, before mincing the meat together.

To make the gelatine:

Clean the pig's feet.

Put them in a saucepan, cover with water and season.

Bring to the boil and then simmer for 2 hours.

To make the pastry:

Put the lard in a saucepan with 1½ pints (900 ml/3 cups) of water. Bring to the boil.

Sieve the flour into a large bowl.

Add the water and lard liquid while still warm, and the melted lard.

Mix together well to make a dough.

Turn on to a floured board and roll out.

Line a large well greased baking tin - a round one is traditional, leaving sufficient pastry to make a lid.

Put the meat in the pie, packing down well.

Place the pastry lid on the top and press the edges together to seal.

Make a slit in the centre to allow the steam to escape.

Brush the top of the pie with the egg wash.

Bake in a moderate oven for about 2½ hours, until a deep golden colour.

Leave until the next day to allow the meat contents to shrink.

Put a pie funnel into the hole in the pie centre and pour in as much warm gelatine as possible.

Allow to set before serving cold with game chips, endive salad, cucumber, tomato, green tomato chutney and Tangy Plum Sauce (see recipe).

Oven: 350°F/180°C   Gas Mark 4

ROAST LEG OF LAMB WITH SCALLIONS AND APRICOTS

1 leg of lamb
8 oz (225 g) dried apricots
8 oz (225 g) scallions or spring onions
1 oz (25 g) sugar
A little fat for roasting

Put the apricots in a bowl, cover with water and leave to soak overnight.

Cut the apricots in half.

Finely chop the spring onions.

Add the sugar to the apricot liquor.

Put the liquid into a saucepan.

Boil rapidly to make a glaze, stirring to dissolve the sugar and prevent burning.

Make incisions on the top of the leg of lamb with a sharp knife at 2 inch (5 cm) intervals.

Fill the slits with the chopped onions and apricot slices.

Brush the glaze all over the skin.

Melt the fat in a roasting tin and seal the meat.

Roast in a moderate oven basting occasionally for 30 minutes per 1 lb (450 g).

Oven: 350°F/180°C   Gas Mark 4

HONEYED WELSH LAMB — Cig Oen â Mêl

This dish has become part of Welsh traditional cooking, and is served at restaurants throughout the country, as well as being popular at the Hwyrnos or Welsh night suppers where local dishes are served by women in attractive regional costume, and musical entertainment is a feature.

4 lbs (1.75 kg) leg or shoulder joint of Welsh lamb
Salt and black pepper
1 teaspoon ginger
1 oz (25 g) rosemary
½ lb (225 g) Welsh honey
½ pint (300 ml/1¼ cups) cider plus a little more if if required

Mix the salt, pepper and ginger together.

Rub into the meat.

Put the joint in a tin foil lined roasting tin — to prevent burning.

Spread the honey evenly over the meat and sprinkle with the rosemary.

Pour the cider into the roasting tin.

Bake for 30 minutes in a hot oven, then in a moderate oven for a further 1½ hours.

Baste from time to time, adding more cider if necessary.

Place the joint on a serving dish.

Skim off any excess fat, and serve the pan juices in a gravy boat as a sauce.

Oven: 400°F/200°C   Gas Mark 6
Reduce to: 325°F/160°C   Gas Mark 3

BONED SADDLE OF LAMB STUFFED WITH BABY LEEKS, WITH ROSEMARY SAUCE

FROM SEIONT MANOR HOTEL   Serves 4

For the boned saddle of lamb:
6 lbs (2.75 kg) of boned loin of lamb (reserve the bones)
1 lb (450 g) baby leeks

For the sauce:
2 lbs (900 g) onions, peeled and roughly diced
1 lb (450 g) tomatoes, roughly diced
A little butter
½ oz (15 g) rosemary

To make the boned saddle of lamb:

If the saddle of lamb has not been boned sufficiently carefully remove any remaining bones with a sharp knife keeping the skin in one piece.

Remove the fillet and loin of lamb in one piece and all fat and sinew from the meat.

Take off the outer leaves of the leeks and blanch in boiling water and refresh in iced water.

Line the fat with leeks overlapping each time.

Wash and blanch the insides of the leeks.

Place the two pieces of loin on the leek lined fat in the middle. Down the centre place the baby leeks, then on top put the lamb fillet. Roll up and tie securely with string.

Roast the lamb in a hot oven for 45 minutes, rest for 5 minutes to allow the juices to re-enter the meat before serving.

To make the sauce:

Chop up some lamb bones into small pieces and roast in the oven until golden brown.

Cook the roughly diced onion and tomatoes in butter.

Combine the bones, onions and tomatoes, add water to cover, and simmer for 1 hour.

Pass through a fine sieve then reduce the sauce by three quarters by boiling over a high heat.

Add the rosemary to the sauce and infuse gently on the stove for 5 minutes.

To serve:

Cut the lamb into four large medallions, then pour on the sauce.

Oven: 425°F/220°C   Gas Mark 7

STUFFED WELSH SHOULDER OF LAMB IN PUFF PASTRY

This recipe comes from the recipe book of Mrs. J. Steventon's grand-mother, who was a professional cook in Ruabon fifty years ago. She grew all her own herbs, and believed that garlic had great medicinal properties, although you may not think her method of 'breathing' on the garlic very hygienic, and prefer to rub the meat over with a clove! The Romans first brought garlic to Wales, where it now grows in great abundance.

1 shoulder of lamb, very lean - boned by the butcher
Garlic
1 lb (450 g) puff pastry
Herb stuffing
Beaten egg

For the herb stuffing:
4 oz (100 g) fresh breadcrumbs
1 teaspoon chopped parsley
1 teaspoon chopped thyme
Grated rind and juice of half a lemon
Salt and black pepper
Beaten egg

Mix the breadcrumbs, parsley, thyme, lemon juice, rind and seasoning together and bind with the beaten egg.

Trim excess fat from the joint.

Fill the cavity where the bone has been removed with the stuffing.

Put a 'breath' of garlic over the joint, by chewing a clove and breathing over it, or rub lightly with a clove.

Roll out the pastry on a floured board, and use to cover the joint.

Lightly score with a knife into a diamond pattern.

Brush with beaten egg.

Cover the joint with tin foil for the first 40 minutes of the cooking time to prevent the pastry browning.

Allow 20 minutes cooking time per lb (450 g) plus an additional 20 minutes.

Cook in a moderately hot oven for first 20 minutes, reducing to moderate for the rest of the cooking time.

Serve hot with vegetables or cold with salad.

Oven: 400°F/200°C   Gas Mark 6
Reduce to: 350°F/180°C   Gas Mark 4

ORANGE LAMB DELIGHT

Serves 4

1 lb (450 g) lamb fillet
Salt and pepper
1 egg, beaten
Dried breadcrumbs to coat
Fat for frying
1 orange, cut into wedges
Watercress to garnish

Cut the lamb fillet into thin strips discarding any fat or sinew.

Season the meat with salt and pepper.

Dip the strips of meat into the beaten egg, then into the breadcrumbs to coat evenly.

Fry in deep fat for five minutes.

Remove the meat and put on a serving dish.

Serve with orange wedges and garnished with watercress.

Squeeze the orange juice over the lamb before eating.

CASSEROLE OF MUTTON CHOPS WITH VEGETABLES

Serves 4

4 mutton chops
2 oz (50 g) butter or margarine
12 young carrots
12 small onions
16 new potatoes
Salt and pepper
½ pint (300 ml/1¼ cups) brown stock
1 dessertspoon flour

Trim the chops and fry them in the butter just sufficiently to brown.

Remove the chops from the frying pan.

Peel and chop the carrots and onions. Peel the potatoes.

Fry the vegetables for a few minutes in the butter.

Remove the vegetables but reserve the butter in the frying pan.

Put the vegetables in an ovenproof casserole, and add the chops.

Season with salt and pepper and pour on the stock.

Cover the casserole and cook in a moderate oven for about 30 minutes until the vegetables and meat are tender.

Remove the casserole from the oven.

Drain and retain the stock.

Stir the flour into the butter in the frying pan, and cook for a few minutes.

Skim off any fat, and gradually add the stock to the flour and butter.

Bring gradually to the boil, stirring, and cook until the gravy thickens.

Put the chops on a hot dish surrounded by the vegetables.

Pour the gravy over the chops before serving.

Oven: 350°F/180°C   Gas Mark 4

WELSH LAMB HOT POT OR LOBSCOUSE

2 breasts of Welsh lamb
1 lb (450 g) onions
1 lb (450 g) potatoes
1 pint (600 ml/2½ cups) stock
Salt and pepper
Mixed herbs to taste

Put the breasts of lamb in a saucepan.

Cover with the stock.

Bring to the boil and gently simmer for 1 hour.

Remove the bones and fat, then strain off the stock.

Peel and slice the potaoes and onions.

Put layers of meat, onions and potatoes, sprinkled with seasoning and mixed herbs into an ovenproof casserole.

Repeat the layers, finishing with potatoes.

Pour on the stock.

Cook in a moderate oven for about 1 hour, or until the vegetables are tender.

Remove the lid for the last 20 minutes of the cooking time to brown the potatoes.

Oven: 350°F/180°C   Gas Mark 4

KATT OR MUTTON PIE

Sweet, spiced mutton pies were popular at the fairs held throughout Wales from the 13th until the early 20th century. The fairs were really large markets often held annually on festivals or saints days. People came from near and far to see and buy livestock, produce and clothing, and to enjoy themselves. Sometimes these events were also hiring fairs, where servants of both sexes could be hired.

Katt Pie was a local speciality for over 200 years at the annual Templeton Fair held in Pembrokeshire on the 12th November. The pastry was traditionally made with suet instead of lard, and the pies were usually made individually, but it is easier in one pie dish.

For the hot water pastry:
1 lb (450 g) plain flour
¼ pint (150 ml/⅔ cup) water or milk and water mixed
2 teaspoons salt
6 oz (175 g) lard

For the mutton pie filling:
12 oz (350 g) mutton or lamb
8 oz (225 g) currants
About 4 oz (100 g) brown sugar
Salt and pepper to taste
Beaten egg or milk to glaze

To make the hot water pastry:

Sift the flour and salt together into a bowl.

Bring the water or milk and water mixed to the boil.

Melt the lard in the water.

Make a well in the dry ingredients and beat in the liquid quickly with a wooden spoon to form a dough.

Knead the dough until smooth.

Cover the bowl with a plate and leave the dough to rest for 20 minutes.

To make the mutton pie:

Roll out the dough on a floured board.

Use about two thirds to line a deep pie dish.

Mince the mutton or lamb.

Fill the pie dish with layers of the meat, seasoned with salt and pepper, currants and brown sugar to taste.

Roll out the remaining pastry to make a lid.

Dampen the edges of the pastry in the pie dish.

Cover with the pastry lid, pressing the edges firmly together to seal.

Make a hole in the top of the pie for the steam to escape.

Brush the top of the pastry over with the beaten egg or milk to glaze.

Bake for 10 minutes in a hot oven. Reduce the temperature and cook for a further 30 minutes until golden brown.

Serve hot.

Oven: 425°F/220°C   Gas Mark 7

Reduce to: 350°F/180°C   Gas Mark 4

CORNED BEEF AND POTATO PIE

This satisfying, economical dish was a family favourite. It was passed down from a mother to her daughter in Mid-Glamorgan, who still makes it to serve with fried potatoes and vegetables. The amounts of corned beef, onion, potatoes and pastry vary according to the size of pie required.

Corned beef
Onion
Potatoes
Salt
About 1 tablespoon of flour
Gravy browning
Shortcrust pastry

Peel and slice the potatoes to about ¼ inch (5 mm) thick.

Chop the onions.

Put the vegetables in a saucepan and cover with water.

Bring to the boil and simmer for about five minutes, just enough to soften the potatoes.

Strain and reserve the cooking liquid.

Add a little salt taking care not to use too much because corned beef is salty.

Slice the corned beef into a pie dish or meat tin according to family size. Mix in a tablespoon of flour.

Pour the vegetable stock over the corned beef and add the gravy browning. Mix until thick gravy forms.

Add the potato and onions.

Roll out the pastry to form a lid. Place the pastry lid on top of the dish.

Cook in a moderately hot oven until the pastry is golden brown.

Oven: 400°F/200°C   Gas Mark 6

SPICED BEEF

3 lbs (1.5 kg) beef brisket or silverside, boned but not
  rolled
4 oz (100 g) coarse salt
1 teaspoon ground nutmeg
1 teaspoon allspice
1 teaspoon ground cloves
½ teaspoon black pepper
2 oz (50 g) brown sugar
½ oz (15 g) saltpetre which can be purchased
  from the chemist
1 tablespoon of black treacle

Rub the salt into the meat and leave overnight.

Take the beef out of the salt and wipe well.

Mix the spices, seasoning, sugar and saltpetre together.

Rub the mixture into the beef on both sides.

Put in a covered bowl and leave in a cool place for two
days.

Evenly pour on the melted treacle.

Turn the meat every day for seven days.

Roll up the meat and secure with string.

Put the spiced beef in a saucepan of boiling water and
simmer for 3 hours.

Spiced beef can be served hot with vegetables but is
especially good if left to get cold in the cooking liquid,
then removed and placed overnight between two flat
plates or boards with a weight on top.

Slice and serve cold.

GALANTINE OF BEEF

1 lb (450 g) shin of beef without bone
Water to cover
Salt and pepper to taste
1 hard-boiled egg
¼ lb (100 g) fat bacon

Dice the meat into small pieces, leaving on any skin, fat and gristle as it helps make a good jelly.

Put the meat into a saucepan, and pour on enough boiling water to barely cover it.

Add salt to taste.

Bring to the boil and simmer gently for 4 hours.

Dice the bacon and add to the meat after 2 hours of cooking time.

Season to taste with a little pepper.

Cut the hard-boiled egg into slices.

Rinse a mould with cold water.

Place the slices of egg at the bottom of the mould.

Put the beef mixture on top and press down well.

Leave overnight to set.

WELSH BEEF STEW —
Cawl Cig Eidion

Serves 8

This recipe is recorded in Eliza Acton's book *Modern Cooking for Private Families* dated 1845.

2½ lbs (1.25 kg) stewing steak
Seasoned flour
1 lb (450 g) leeks
1 lb (450 g) onions
12 oz (350 g) turnips
Fat for frying
2 pints (1.15 litres/4 cups) brown stock
1 teaspoon of sugar
Salt and pepper

Cut the meat into cubes and roll in the seasoned flour.

Wash and chop the leeks, and peel and slice the onions and turnips.

Heat a little fat in a large saucepan and fry the meat to seal on all sides, and the onions until golden brown.

Gradually pour on the stock and add the chopped leeks, turnips, sugar and seasoning.

Bring to the boil, then put the lid on the saucepan and simmer for about 2½ hours.

If preferred, the stew can be cooked in a casserole dish in a moderate oven for 2½ hours.

Oven: 325°F/160°C   Gas Mark 3

Beef with Cabbage Sauce

From Eliza Sloughter's recipe book dated 1771.

'You must simmer a brisket of beef six hours as white as possible then boil some young cabbage and pulp them through a sieve then mix half a pint of cream a lump of butter a little pepper and salt pour it over the beef when it goes to table.'

BACON RIBS AND CABBAGE   Serves 3-4

Bacon ribs (allow 4 per person)
1 hard white cabbage
2 medium onions
A knob of butter
Salt and pepper

Wash the bacon ribs well.

Put them in a saucepan of boiling water and simmer until the meat comes away from the bone.

Shred the cabbage finely.

Peel and slice the onions.

Put the onion and cabbage into a separate saucepan with a little water and a knob of butter.

Cover and steam until the vegetables are tender.

Strain and season with salt and pepper.

Put the vegetables into a serving dish making a bed to put the bacon pieces on.

BACON RIBS WITH BROAD BEAN SAUCE

Allow four lean bacon ribs per person.   Serves 4

16 bacon ribs
2 lbs (900 g) broad beans
1 pint (600 ml/2½ cups) white sauce

For the white sauce:
1 oz (25 g) butter or margarine
1 oz (25 g) flour
1 pint (600 ml/2½ cups) milk
Salt and pepper

Put the bacon ribs in a saucepan and cover them with water.

Bring to the boil.

Drain.

Cover with fresh water, bring to the boil again and simmer for 2 hours.

Shell the beans, and put them in the saucepan with the ribs for 8-10 minutes before the end of the bacon cooking time.

To make the white sauce:

Melt the fat in a saucepan.

Stir in the flour and cook gently for 2-3 minutes, stirring continuously.

Gradually add the milk and bring to the boil, still stirring.

Simmer until the sauce thickens, and season to taste.

To serve:

Drain the beans and the bacon.

Add the cooked beans to the white sauce, and pour over the ribs before serving.

LEEK AND BACON DUFF
WITH PARSLEY SAUCE

Serves 4

For the leek and bacon duff:
4 leeks
8 oz (225 g) smoked streaky bacon rashers
1 lb (450 g) suet pastry
A good pinch of dried sage
Salt and pepper

For the savoury suet duff or pastry:
8 oz (225 g) plain flour
4 oz (100 g) chopped suet
A pinch of salt
¼ pint (150 ml/⅔ cup) cold water

For the parsley sauce:
½ pint (300 ml/1¼ cups) white sauce
1 teaspoon parsley
Salt and pepper

To make the savoury suet duff or pastry:

Mix the flour, suet and salt together with the cold water to make a stiff dough.

To make the leek and bacon duff:

Wash and slice the leeks.

Take the rinds off the rashers, and chop the bacon.

Roll out the pastry on a floured board to an oblong shape about ¼ inch (1 cm) thick.

Put the sliced leeks evenly on the pastry, leaving the edges free.

Sprinkle generously with dried sage and seasoning.

Cover with the chopped bacon.

Dampen the edges with cold water.

Roll up, pressing the edges together to seal.

Put the pudding in a floured linen or cotton cloth, or tin foil, and tie well.

Steam for 2 hours.

Remove the pudding carefully from the cloth and serve sliced with parsley sauce.

To make the parsley sauce:

Wash the parsley, dry well to ensure even distribution throughout the sauce, and chop finely.

Bring the white sauce to boiling point, lower the temperature and stir in the parsley.

Season to taste with salt and pepper.

THE MISER'S FEAST — Ffest y Cybydd

This is an old Carmarthenshire recipe. It was said that the miser would eat the potatoes one day, mashed up in the liquid, and keep the slices of bacon for the next day with plain boiled potatoes. The actual amount of the ingredients depended upon what was available.

Potatoes
Onions
Salt and pepper
Some slices of Welsh bacon

Peel and slice some potatoes and onions.

Starting with the potatoes, put layers of the vegetables in a saucepan.

Cover with water, and season with salt and pepper.

Put some slices of bacon on top.

Cover and simmer until the potatoes are cooked, when most of the liquid will be absorbed.

SAVOURY FAGGOTS — Ffagodau   Serves 4

This dish, formerly traditionally made at pig-killing time, is still popular served hot with green peas. Ready-made faggots can be bought at butcher's shops.

1 lb (450 g) pig's liver
4 lb (100 g) fat bacon or belly pork
½ lb (225 g) onions
½ lb (225 g) breadcrumbs
Salt and pepper
1 teaspoon powdered sage
A little flour
A caul or apron
½ - ¾ pint (300 ml/1¼ cups or 450 ml/2 cups) brown stock

Mince the liver with belly pork and onions into a bowl.

Add the breadcrumbs, seasoning and sage.

Mix well together and form into balls.

Toss these in flour and pack closely into a baking tin.

Dip the caul or apron into warm water and stretch gently.

Cut into pieces and use to cover each faggot.

Cover the baking tin with tin foil.

Bake in a moderate oven for 30-40 minutes, making sure the dish does not become dry.

Oven: 350°F/180°C   Gas Mark 4

LIVER AND ONION CASSEROLE   Serves 4

This liver and onion stew was traditionally served with stwn —
potatoes mashed together with another vegetable, and was popular in
North Wales.

1 lb (450 g) lamb or calf's liver
1 lb (450 g) onions
2 oz (50 g) flour
Fat for frying
Salt and pepper
½ pint (300 ml/1¼ cups) brown stock

Trim and cut the liver into slices.

Peel and slice the onions.

Season the flour with the salt and pepper, and roll the
liver slices in it.

Heat the fat in a frying pan and lightly fry the liver on
both sides, and the onions until transparent.

Put the liver and onions in a casserole, and pour on the
stock.

Add more seasoning if required.

Cover the casserole with a lid or foil.

Bake in a moderate oven for 45-60 minutes or until
tender.

Oven: 350°F/180°C   Gas Mark 4

PRESELY PIE — Pastai Preseli

Serves 4

This dish originated in the Presely Hills area which is rich in prehistoric remains and is said to be the location for some of the stones used in the famous circle at Stonehenge in Wiltshire.

½ lb (225 g) shortcrust pastry
4 oz (100 g) cooked meat
1 lb (450 g) cooked mashed potato
4 oz (100 g) bacon
1 medium or 2 small onions
1 teaspoon dried sage
Salt and pepper
Thick brown gravy

Roll out the pastry on a floured board.

Use to line a greased ovenproof pie dish.

Bake 'blind' for about 15 minutes until lightly browned.

Dice the meat.

Peel and finely chop the onion.

Chop the bacon and fry in a saucepan until the fat runs.

Add the onion and fry until soft.

Stir in the meat, mashed potato, sage and seasoning to taste.

Continue stirring until the mixture is thoroughly heated through.

Pile the mixture into the pastry case.

Bake in a moderate oven for about 10 minutes until golden brown.

Serve with thick brown gravy.

Oven: 450°F/230°C   Gas Mark 8
Reduce to: 350°F/180°C   Gas Mark 4

LEEK PASTY — Pastai Cennin

Serves 2 or 3

8 oz (225 g) shortcrust pastry
2 or 3 medium sized leeks
4 rashers of streaky bacon
Salt and pepper

Wash and finely chop the leeks.

Line a greased baking plate (about the size of a dinner plate) or shallow pie dish with half the pastry.

Cover the pastry with the leeks, leaving the edges free.

Remove the rinds from the bacon, and lay it in strips on top of the leeks.

Season with salt and pepper to taste.

Moisten the mixture with 1 tablespoonful of cold water, and also dampen the edges of the pastry.

Roll out the rest of the pastry to form a lid.

Use to cover the pastry, pressing the edges together to seal.

Make a slit in the top to allow the steam to escape.

Bake in a moderate hot oven for about 35 minutes until golden brown.

Oven: 400°F/200°C   Gas Mark 6

WINTER HASTY LEEKS

Serves 6

An economical dish particularly suitable for a cold day.

9 leeks
2 lbs (900 g) potatoes
Salt
A little butter
6 rashers streaky bacon
1 pint (600 m/2½ cups) white sauce

For the white sauce:
1 oz (25 g) butter or margarine
1 oz (25 g) flour
1 pint (600 ml/2½ cups) milk
Salt and pepper

To make the white sauce:

Melt the fat in a saucepan.

Stir in the flour and cook without browning for 2 or 3 minutes.

Add the milk gradually, stirring continuously.

Bring to the boil, and simmer, still stirring, until the sauce thickens.

Season with salt and pepper to taste.

To make the leek dish:

Wash and slice the leeks.

Peel and chop the potatoes.

Put in two saucepans of salted water.

Bring to the boil and simmer until tender.

Drain. Mash the potatoes with the butter until well creamed, and pipe the potatoes round the sides of a greased ovenproof dish.

Fill the centre with the cooked leeks.

Pour over the white sauce.

Grill the bacon until crispy.

Cut into pieces and arrange on top of the dish.

Brown in the oven before serving.

LEEK PORRIDGE

Serves 6

12 leeks
Salt and pepper
6 rounds of buttered toast

Take off the outside leaves of the leeks, but leave the rest whole.

Clean thoroughly.

Put in a saucepan with sufficient cold water to cover.

Season with salt and pepper.

Bring to the boil and simmer for about 10 minutes until tender.

Strain, reserving the cooking liquid.

Cut the leeks into thin slices, and put them into six porridge bowls.

Moisten each portion with a little of the cooking liquid.

Serve hot with freshly made buttered toast cut into fingers.

LEEKIE PIE

The leek which is used in so many of the country's recipes, is the national emblem of Wales.

6 oz (175 g) or more, of leeks
½ lb (225 g) shortcrust pastry
2 tablespoons meat stock
1 egg
Salt and pepper
2 oz (50 g) grated cheese (optional)

Wash and cut the leeks into small pieces.

Drop them into a saucepan of boiling salted water.

Simmer for 10 minutes and then strain.

Roll out the pastry and use half to line a deep greased ovenproof plate.

Place the leeks on the pastry, and pour over 2 tablespoons of meat stock and the well beaten egg.

Season with salt and pepper and sprinkle with grated cheese.

Moisten the edges of the pastry with a little water.

Roll out the rest of the pastry to make a lid and use to cover the pie.

Press the edges together to seal.

Make a slit in the top to allow the steam to escape.

Bake in a moderate oven for 25-30 minutes until golden brown.

Serve hot.

Oven: 350°F/180°C   Gas Mark 4

JACKET POTATOES WITH LEEK
AND BACON FILLING

Serves 4

4 potatoes suitable for baking

For the filling:
2 leeks
4 rashers of streaky bacon
½ pint (300 ml/1¼ cups) white sauce (see page 52)
A little grated cheese
Paprika

Wash the potatoes and prick them with a fork.

Bake in a moderately hot oven for about 1 hour, depending on size.

To make the filling:

Wash and slice the leeks.

Put in a saucepan with a little boiling salted water.

Simmer for about five minutes until tender.

Fry or grill the bacon and cut into small pieces.

Drain the leeks and stir gently into the hot white sauce, with the bacon.

To serve:

Remove the potatoes from the oven, score the top with a knife into a cross.

Press the sides of the potato to open it.

Fill with the leek and bacon filling mixture.

Sprinkle with grated cheese and a dash of paprika.

Oven: 400°F/200°C   Gas Mark 6

POTATO CAKES — Teisennau Tatws

Makes about 10 cakes

Potato cakes were traditionally served with a glass of buttermilk.

8 oz (225 g) potatoes
2 oz (50 g) butter or margarine
1 egg, well beaten
2-3 oz (50-75 g) flour
1 teaspoon salt
A pinch of cinnamon
1 teaspoon of baking powder
Milk to mix

Peel and boil the potatoes.

Mash well with a fork or put through a sieve.

Blend in the butter, and the egg.

Mix the flour, salt, cinnamon and baking powder together in a bowl.

Stir the dry ingredients into the potato mixture.

Mix with milk to a stiff consistency.

Turn on to a floured board, and knead lightly.

Roll and cut or form by hand into 1 inch (2.5 cm) flat cakes.

Bake the cakes on a griddle on both sides, or place on a greased baking tray in a hot oven for about 20 minutes until golden brown.

Serve hot, split open and buttered.

Alternatively the cakes can be fried and served with bacon, egg and laverbread.

ONION CAKE — Teisen Nionod   Serves 4 - 6

This traditional Welsh dish probably got its name because it was always made in a cake tin and turned out before serving. A round ovenproof dish makes an acceptable alternative.

1½ lbs (675 g) potatoes
3 onions
Salt and pepper
2 oz (50 g) butter or margarine

Peel and slice the potatoes.

Peel and chop the onions.

Put a layer of potatoes in a greased cake tin or ovenproof dish.

Season with salt and pepper to taste.

Add a layer of chopped onions and dot with butter or margarine.

Repeat these layers until the dish is full, finishing with potatoes, well dotted with butter.

Cover with a lid or foil and bake in a moderate oven for one hour.

Turn out and serve with hot or cold meat.

Oven: 350°F/180°C   Gas Mark 4

STWNS

Stwn is a popular Welsh dish made by mashing potatoes together with other vegetables. Peas, broad beans or swedes can be used instead of turnips. Stwn was traditionally served in North Wales with a liver and onion stew.

8 oz(225 g) potatoes
8 oz (225 g) young turnips
2 oz (50 g) butter or margarine
Salt and pepper to taste
Buttermilk to mix or serve

Peel and chop the potatoes and turnips.

Put the vegetables in a saucepan of boiling salted water.

Simmer for about 20 minutes until tender.

Drain and mash together.

Add the butter and seasoning to taste.

Mix with the buttermilk to a creamy consistency, or pour the buttermilk over the stwn before serving.

A Potato Pudding

From Eliza Sloughter's recipe book dated 1771.

'Take a half a pound of potatoes after being boiled and beat very fine, six ounces of sugar, four eggs, the juice of a lemon with the peel grated in half a pound of butter a little ratafin or brandy. Bake it with a paste round the dish.'

PUNCHNEP

The name of this delicious vegetable dish derives from the old pronounciation of turnip and parsnip which was parsnep and turnep. It is excellent served with either grilled or roast meat.

1 lb (450 g) potatoes
1 lb (450 g) young white turnips
About 2 oz (50 g) butter or margarine
Salt and pepper to taste
2½ fl oz (4 tablespoons/⅓ cup) cream

Peel and slice the potatoes and turnips.

Put them into separate saucepans of salted water.

Bring to the boil, and simmer until tender.

Drain and mash throughly adding about 1 oz (25 g) butter to each vegetable, or a little more if preferred.

Add pepper to taste and check the seasoning.

Mix the potatoes and turnips together, beat to a smooth cream.

Put into a serving dish, pressing the mixture down and smoothing the top.

Make several holes down through the mixture with a skewer.

Keep hot.

Gently warm the cream, and pour it into the holes.

BOILED ONIONS

Serves 4

4 large onions of similar size
2 oz (50 g) butter or margarine
Salt and pepper
1 tablespoon chopped parsley

Peel the onions.

Put them in a saucepan of boiling salted water.

Simmer for about 30 minutes until tender.

Drain well, and put in a serving dish.

Serve with a knob of butter in the centre of each onion, sprinkled with chopped parsley.

How to Make Artechoak Pie

From Rebekah Jones, her book, dated 1740

'Take the bottom of Artechoaks being boiled very tender put them in a dish and put some vinegar over them season them with ginger and sugar a little mace whole putting them into a pie and when you lay them in lay in some marrow and dates sliced in and a few raisins of the sun in the bottom with good store of butter so close the pie when it is halfe baked take a dish of sack being boiled first with sugar and a pill of orange. put it in your pie and set it in the oven again till you use it.'

WELSH RAREBIT — Caws Pobi   Serves 4

Welsh rarebit is one of the most well known of cheese dishes and is also popular throughout Great Britain.

White wine may be used instead of beer or milk.
Buck Rarebit can be made by serving with a poached egg on top.

8 oz (225 g) grated cheese
1 oz (25 g) butter or margarine
2 tablespoons of milk or beer
2 eggs, beaten
4 tablespoons of breadcrumbs
Salt and pepper
½ teaspoon of dry mustard
4 slices of bread, toasted one side only

Melt the butter in a saucepan.

Add the milk or beer, egg, grated cheese, breadcrumbs and seasonings.

Cook slowly over a gentle heat for a few minutes until the cheese has melted and the sauce has thickened.

Spread the cheese mixture on to the untoasted side of the bread.

Brown under the grill and serve hot.

WELSH CHEESE PUDDING —
Pwdin Caws Cymru

Serves 6

6 thick slices of bread
Butter for spreading
1½ pints (900 ml/3¾ cups) milk
2 eggs
12 oz (300 g) grated cheese
Salt and pepper
1 teaspoon of nutmeg
1 teaspoon of dry mustard

Cut the crusts off the bread.

Toast one side of each piece of bread only and butter it.

Fit 3 pieces of the bread, toasted side down, in the bottom of a large greased, ovenproof dish.

Sprinkle with half the cheese.

Put the other pieces of bread on top, buttered side up and sprinkle with the remaining cheese.

Heat the milk but do not boil

Beat in the egg and seasonings.

Pour over the bread and leave the milk to soak into the bread about 20-30 minutes.

Bake in a moderately hot oven for about 30 minutes or until well risen and golden brown on top.

Oven: 350°F/180°C   Gas Mark 4

TROLLIES

Trollies or 'trolls' are small suet puddings, sometimes made with oatmeal and boiled in the cawl or broth. A sweet version, like this, is also made and served with sugar and butter.

8 oz (225 g) flour
1 teaspoon of baking powder
3 oz (75 g) suet
A pinch of salt
Milk for mixing
1 teaspoon cinnamon
3 oz (75 g) raisins
2 oz (50 g) demerara sugar
Flour for coating
Sugar, butter and cream for serving

Mix the flour, baking powder, suet and salt together.

Mix to a stiff paste with a little milk.

Roll out on a floured surface, and cut into squares.

Sprinkle a few raisins, a little sugar and a pinch of cinnamon in the centre of each square.

Fold over and then form into balls.

Coat each ball with flour and drop individually into a pan of boiling water.

Cook for about 15-20 minutes.

Serve with a sprinkling of sugar and a knob of butter on each. If liked, whipped cream can also be added.

BLACKBERRY PUDDING

Serves 4

This pudding can be made with blackberry jam if blackberries are not available.

4 oz (100 g) blackberries
4 oz (100 g) self-raising flour
3 oz (75 g) suet
1 oz (25 g) sugar
1 teaspoon of bicarbonate of soda
A pinch of salt
5 or 6 tablespoons of milk
2 tablespoons of blackberry jam, melted

Mix the dry ingredients together.

Add the blackberries.

Bind the ingredients together with the milk.

Pour into a greased pudding basin.

Cover the top with greaseproof paper and a cloth, securely tied.

Steam in a pan of boiling water for 2 hours.

Do not allow the pan to boil dry.

Heat the jam until it melts and serve with the pudding.

MONMOUTH PUDDING —
Pwdin Mynwy

Serves 3 - 4

8 oz (225 g) breadcrumbs
1 lemon rind grated
½ pint (300 ml/1¼ cups) milk
2 oz (50 g) sugar
1 oz (25 g) butter
3 eggs separated
½ lb (225 g) raspberry jam

Put the breadcrumbs in a bowl with the grated lemon rind.

Bring the milk to boiling point and pour over the breadcrumbs.

Cover the basin and leave for 10-15 minutes to stand.

Blend the sugar, butter and beaten egg yolks together.

Whisk the egg whites until they are stiff and fold them into the breadcrumb mixture.

Grease an ovenproof dish and spread a layer of jam over the bottom.

Pour over half the breadcrumb mixture.

Repeat with a layer of jam and a layer of breadcrumbs.

Bake in a moderate oven for about 30 minutes or until the pudding is set.

Oven: 325°F/160°C   Gas Mark 3

SNOWDON PUDDING —
Pwdin Eryri

A steamed suet pudding that was eaten at the hotel at the foot of Mount Snowdon, this was especially popular with hungry climbers and was served with a mulled wine sauce.

3 oz (75 g) seedless raisins
4 oz (100 g) suet
4 oz (100 g) breadcrumbs
3 oz (75 g) brown sugar
1 tablespoon cornflour
A pinch of salt
Grated rind of a lemon
3 eggs
1 tablespoon of marmalade

For the sauce:
½ pint (300 ml/1¼ cups) red wine
4 oz (100 g) sugar
The rind of half a lemon

Butter a round pudding basin.

Cover the sides of the basin with some of the raisins.

Mix together the suet, breadcrumbs, sugar, cornflour, salt and remaining raisins.

Add the grated lemon rind and the well beaten egg and finally the marmalade.

Pour the mixture carefully into the basin so that the raisins are left on the sides.

Do not fill the basin to the top so that the pudding has room to rise.

Cover the top with greaseproof paper and a cloth, securely tied.

Boil the pudding in a pan of boiling water for about an hour. Do not allow to boil dry.

To make the sauce:

Simmer the wine, sugar and whole lemon rind in a pan until the sugar dissolves and the liquid is reduced and syrupy.

Remove the lemon rind and serve hot with the pudding.

WELSH PUDDING

8 oz (225 g) shortcrust pastry
2 tablespoons raspberry jam
4 oz (100 g) butter
4 oz (100 g) sugar
2 eggs
4 oz (100 g) plain flour
½ teaspoon baking powder

Line a shallow greased ovenproof dish with the pastry.

Spread a layer of jam on the bottom.

Cream together the butter and sugar.

Beat in the eggs.

Sift the flour and the baking powder and fold it into the mixture.

Pour into the dish and bake in a moderately hot oven for about 30 minutes.

Serve hot with raspberry custard or melted raspberry jam.

Oven: 375°F/190°C   Gas Mark 5

BAKESTONE FRUIT TART OR TURNOVER

This recipe makes a quick and easy fruit turnover which was made on a bakestone. A similar but larger version, served at harvest time and known as Harvest Cake, was made with wafer-thin pastry, filled with puréed fruit, cut into squates and eaten with a glass of buttermilk.

½ lb (225 g) shortcrust pastry
½ lb (225 g) cooked fruit such as apples, blackberries, rhubarb or gooseberries
1 oz (25 g) brown sugar
1 oz (25 g) butter or margarine

Roll out the pastry on a floured surface and make a round.

Cover one half with the fruit.

Fold the pastry over the fruit, dampen the edges and seal them.

Using a wooden pastry slice gently lift the turnover on to a heated greased bakestone. A heavy frying pan may be used instead.

Cook slowly until each side is golden brown.

Remove the pastry and sprinkle the top with sugar.
and small pieces of butter or margarine.

Almond Cheese Cake

'Four of sweet and two of bitter almonds blanched and pound very fine, nine oz of loaf sugar beat and sifted, two spoonfuls of brandy, whites of 4 eggs beat to a stiff froth, mix them together, have ready a light puff paste* in your tins that they may not stand or they will be heavy.'

*Pastry

WELSH CHEESE CAKES

Makes about 12

Cheesecakes were a farmhouse speciality made with curd cheese. During later centuries the cheese has been substituted but the name still remains. Welsh Cheesecakes are filled with jam.

This recipe was a prize winner in an anual competition usually held on St. David's Day and involving pupils at comprehensive schools throughout Wales.

½ lb (225 g) shortcrust pastry
2 tablespoons raspberry jam

For the filling:
2 oz (50 g) butter or margarine
2 oz (50 g) caster sugar
1 egg
3 oz (75 g) self-raising flour

Roll out the pastry on a floured surface.

Line the greased patty tins.

Put a small teaspoon of jam in each.

Cream together the butter and sugar.

Beat in the egg.

Fold in the flour.

Put about a dessertspoon of the mixture over the jam in each, and bake in a moderately hot oven for about 15 minutes or until well risen and golden brown.

Oven: 375°F/190°C   Gas Mark 5

LEMON PIE

8 oz (225 g) shortcrust pastry
1 oz (25 g) butter
4 oz (100 g) sugar
2 eggs, separated
Grated rind of a lemon
Juice of half a lemon
4 fl oz (6 tablespoons/½ cup) milk

Roll out the pastry on a floured surface and use to lined a greased tart dish.

Cream together the butter and the sugar.

Add the well beaten egg yolks, the lemon rind and the milk.

Whisk the egg whites stiffly and fold them into the lemon mixture.

Pour into the pastry and bake for 30 minutes in a moderate oven.

Alternatively the lemon mixture can be allowed to cool and poured into sundae glasses and served with whipped cream.

Oven: 350°F/180°C   Gas Mark 4

MARROW AND APPLE PIE

Pumpkin may be used instead of marrow and apple. Pumpkins were grown in the Gower peninsula and eaten in many ways, pumpkin pie being one of them.

1 lb (450 g) shortcrust pastry
1 small marrow
½ lb (225 g) cooking apples
4 oz (100 g) sugar
3 oz (75 g) currants
½ teaspoon ginger
2 or 3 cloves

Roll out half the pastry on a floured surface and use to line a deep pie dish.

Peel and slice the marrow, removing the seeds.

Peel, core and slice the apples.

Fill the pie dish with a layer of marrow and a layer of apple.

Sprinkle with sugar, currants and the spices.

Roll out the remaining pastry and use to cover the pie.

Bake in a moderate oven for about 40 - 45 minutes until the pastry is golden brown.

Oven: 325°F/160°C   Gas Mark 3

How to Make a Tart of Rice

A hand written recipe dating from 1740 for a delicious spicy rice tart.

'Boil your rice and then season it with cinnamon nutmeg ginger pepper and sugar the yolks of three or four eggs then put it into your tart with the juice of one orange then close it bake it and ice it scrape on sugar and serve it.'

EGG WHEY — Maidd yr Iâr

1 pint (600 ml/2½ cups) milk
1 egg, beaten
A knob of butter
1 tablespoon of sugar
1 teaspoon of syrup
A pinch of salt
2 thick slices of bread

Heat the milk to almost boiling point.

Add the beaten egg, butter, sugar, syrup and salt.

Heat through over a gentle heat.

Break the bread into an ovenproof dish and pour over the milk mixture.

Bake in the oven until set.

Oven: 300°C/150°F   Gas Mark 2

LEMON AND ELDERFLOWER SORBET

Another favourite recipe from the White Horse Inn, Llandeilo.

4 lemons
4 elderflower heads
1 lb (450 g) caster sugar
3 egg whites
4 pints (2.25 litres/8 cups) water
Lemon balm to decorate

Wash and slice the lemons and place in a large heavy based saucepan.

Wash the elderflower heads and add to the pan,

Add the water and heat gently for 10-15 minutes, then boil for 5 minutes.

Strain the liquid into a clean pan, and stir in the sugar over a low heat until it dissolves.

Allow to cool, then fast freeze until slushy.

Remove from the freezer and whisk by hand or in an electric blender.

Return to the freezer for 30 minutes or so until slushy again.

Whisk the egg whites until stiff and add to the sorbet.

Whisk again and return the mixture to the freezer until firm. The more you whisk the sorbet, the better the texture will be.

Serve decorated with lemon balm.

HONEY CAKE — Teisen Fêl

Until the end of the 19th century girls would bring honey cakes to King Aurthur's Stone at the top of Cefn Lefn, Bryn Common. They believed that if they placed the cakes on the stone and then crawled round it three times, their true loves would appear.

Honeycake is a sweet spicy cake with a meringue topping that can also be served as a pudding. It can be made into small individual cakes without a meringue topping but with a light sprinkling of sugar instead.

8 oz (225 g) plain flour
½ teaspoon bicarbonate of soda
1 teaspoon cinnamon
4 oz (100 g) butter
4 oz (100 g) sugar
1 egg separated
6 tablespoons honey, warmed
3-4 tablespoons milk

For the topping:
1 tablespoon of warmed honey
2 egg whites
2 tablespoons caster sugar

Sift together the flour, bicarbonate of soda and cinnamon.

Cream the butter with the sugar.

Separate the egg and beat in the egg yolk.

Add the warmed honey, a little at a time.

Blend in the flour and enough milk to make a soft dropping consistency.

Whisk the egg white until frothy and fold it into the mixture.

Pour the mixture into a greased tin.

Bake in a hot oven for 20-30 minutes.

Leave it to cool a little and then remove the cake from the tin to cool further.

Brush a layer of honey over the top of the cake.

Whisk the egg whites until stiff and add the caster sugar to make a meringue.

Spread the meringue over the top of the cake.

Carefully place the cake on a baking tray and return to a cooler oven for a few minutes until the meringue turns golden brown.

If eaten as a pudding, serve with plenty of whipped cream.

Oven: 400°F/200°C   Gas Mark 6
Reduce to: 325°F/160°C   Gas Mark 3

A Very Good Common Cake

'Two pounds of flour one pound of butter eight eggs half a pint of good milk and four spoonfuls of yeast, mix all together, let it stand to rise, then work in a quarter of a pound of fine moist sugar, half a pound of currants well cleaned and four ounces of candied lemon put it into a tin bake one hour.'

RHUBARB CAKE

9 oz (250 g) self-raising flour
3 oz (75 g) butter or margarine
4 oz (100 g) sugar
8 oz (225 g) rhubarb
1 large egg, beaten
4 tablespoons milk

Rub the fat into the flour until it resembles fine bread-crumbs.

Add the sugar and the finely cubed rhubarb.

Beat in the egg and the milk to make a soft dough.

Turn the mixture on to a greased baking tin and bake for about an hour until the cake stops 'sizzling' and the rhubarb looks more like sultanas.

Oven: 350°F/180°C   Gas Mark 4

PLATE CAKE — Teisen Lap

Teisen lap, meaning literally plate cake, is traditionally made through-out Wales. It can be cooked in a shallow tin or an ovenproof plate or rolled out to an overall thickness of 1 inch (2.5 cm) and cooked on a bakestone or griddle until brown on each side. This cake keeps well if kept in an airtight container, or wrapped in foil.

8 oz (225 g) self-raising flour
2 oz (50 g) butter or margarine
2 oz (50 g) lard
4 oz (100 g) sugar
½ teaspoon grated nutmeg
4 oz (100 g) mixed dry fruit
2 eggs beaten
¼ pint (150 ml/⅔cup) milk or buttermilk

Put the flour in a bowl.

Rub the fat into the flour until the mixture resembles fine breadcrumbs.

Add the sugar, nutmeg and dried fruit.

Mix in the eggs and enough of the milk to make a soft dropping consistency.

Beat well and place the mixture in a shallow tin or plate and bake in a moderate oven for 20 minutes reducing to cool for 30-40 minutes.

Test with a skewer to ensure the cake is cooked right through before removing from the oven. The skewer should come out clean.

Turn out and cool.

Sprinkle with caster sugar.

Oven: 350°F/180°C   Gas Mark 4
Reduce to: 300°F/150°C   Gas Mark 2

POTATO CAKE — Teisen Datws

Potato Cakes - a basic mixture of cooked mashed potato, flour and spices, were popular in the last century. There are variations such as pastry parcels with sweet fillings of apples, sugar and ginger, or savoury fillings with cheese.

1 lb (450 g) cooked mashed potato
8 oz (225 g) self-raising flour
4 oz (100 g) sugar
4 oz (100 g) mixed dried fruit such as sultanas
A good pinch of cinnamon and mixed spice
Milk to mix

Mix the dry ingredients together.

Add sufficient milk to mix to a stiff consistency.

Put the mixture into a greased shallow baking tin.

Cook in a moderate oven for 45 minutes to an hour or until the top of the cake is firm.

Leave the cake to cool in the tin.

Cut into 2 inch (5 cm) fingers.

Oven: 350°F/180°C   Gas Mark 4

SHEARING CAKE — Cacen Cneifio

Hill farming is a traditional way of life for the Welsh farmer and one of the most arduous times is shearing. In the past it would involve the community as a whole and a special cake, aptly named Shearing Cake, was baked to celebrate the work being completed. It is a delicious cake which is still enjoyed today.

8 oz (225 g) wholemeal flour
8 oz (225 g) plain flour
1 teaspoon baking powder
8 oz (225 g) butter or margarine
A pinch of salt
1 teaspoon ground nutmeg
1 tablespoon caraway seeds
The grated rind and juice of one lemon
2 eggs, beaten
½ pint (300 ml/1¼ cups) milk

Sieve the flour with the baking powder.

Rub the fat into the flour until it resembles fine breadcrumbs.

Add the sugar, caraway seeds, salt, nutmeg, lemon rind and juice and mix the ingredients together well.

Gradually add the egg and the milk and beat until well blended.

Pour the mixture into a greased 9 inch (23 cm) square cake tin.

Cook in a moderate oven for about 30 minutes, then reduce to a slow oven for about 1½ hours.

Oven: 350°F/180°C   Gas Mark 4
Reduce to: 300°F/150°C   Gas Mark 2

SPECKLED CAKE — Cacen-Gri

Serves 4

Cacen-Gri, spread with plenty of butter, is reported to have been one of Lloyd George's favourite dishes.

8 oz (225 g) plain flour
1 teaspoon of baking powder
4 oz (100 g) butter or margarine
1 oz (25 g) sugar
1 oz (25 g) currants
1 egg beaten
A little milk

Sieve the flour with the baking powder.

Add the sugar and the currants.

Mix in the beaten egg and enough milk to make a stiff dough.

Roll out thinly on a floured surface.

Divide into rounds and cook on a greased bakestone, griddle or heavy frying pan.

Cook the rounds until golden brown on each side.

Butter and serve hot.

ANGLESEY CAKE — Teisen Sir Fôn

6 oz (175 g) flour
2 oz (50 g) butter
2 oz (50 g) sugar
1 egg beaten
2 oz (50 g) mixed dried fruit
½ teaspoon of baking powder
A little milk for mixing

Rub the butter into the flour.

Mix in the sugar, baking powder, beaten egg and the fruit.

Add the little milk if needed to form a soft dropping consistency but the mixture should not be too wet.

Put the cake mixture into a buttered sandwich tin and bake in a moderately hot oven for 30-40 minutes.

Eat hot with butter.

Oven: 375°F/190°C   Gas Mark 5

HUISH CAKE

4 oz (100 g) self-raising flour
4 oz (100 g) ground rice
4 oz (100 g) butter
8 oz (225 g) caster sugar
4 eggs separated
Caraway seeds to taste

Mix together the flour and the rice.

Cream the butter and sugar together.

Blend in the egg yolks.

Add the flour mixture and caraway seeds.

Whisk the egg whites until frothy and fold into the mixture.

Pour into a well greased cake tin and bake for about 45 minutes.

Oven: 400°F/200°C   Gas Mark 6

SODA CAKE

A very good cake.

1 lb (450 g) flour
6 oz (175 g) butter
8 oz (225 g) dried fruit such as currants and raisins
½ oz (15 g) ground cinnamon
2 eggs, well beaten
1 teaspoon of bicarbonate soda
5 or 6 tablespoons of milk

Rub the butter into the flour.

Add the fruit and spices, mixing well.

Blend in the beaten eggs.

Mix the soda with a little of the milk and mix in the rest of the milk.

Beat the ingredients well together.

Put the mixture in a greased tin and bake for about 1½ hours.

Oven: 350°F/180°C   Gas Mark 4

CAT CRISPIES

2 oz (50 g) icing sugar
4 oz (100 g) butter
8 oz (225 g) rolled oats
1 oz (25 g) desiccated coconut

Rub the sugar through a fine sieve.

Put the butter in a warm place to make it creamy without letting it oil.

Then cream the butter with the sugar.

Knead in the oats and the coconut and salt.

Continue kneading to a thick paste.

Break off small pieces and roll into balls.

Place the balls on a greased baking tin.

Press each with a fork to flatten a little and bake in a moderate oven for 30-40 minutes.

Oven: 325°F/160°C   Gas Mark 3

LADY BETTY WARBURTON'S BISCUIT CAKE

This cake was originally made by the cook of a large household.

'Take the yolks of twelve eggs, beat them by themselves whilst another person whisks up the whites of six eggs to a froth, have ready three quarters of a pound of sugar beat and sifted, put to it the yolks of the eggs and then the whites beat them well together for an hour then stir in half a pound of fine flour and grated lemon peel to your taste, bake it in a tin, when baked through turn it out.'

CARAWAY BISCUITS

A Welsh favourite.

12 oz (350 g) flour
4 oz (100 g) butter
4 oz (100 g) sugar
½ teaspoon caraway seeds or to taste
A little cold water for mixing

Rub the fat into the flour until the mixture resembles fine breadcrumbs.

Add the sugar and the caraway seeds and mix well.

Add enough water to make a stiff dough.

Roll out the dough on a floured surface to about ¼ inch (5 mm) thick.

Cut 3 inch (7.5 cm) rounds and place them on a well buttered baking sheet.

Prick the biscuits well with a fork and bake in a moderate oven for about 20 minutes.

Oven: 350°F/180°C   Gas Mark 4

ABERFFRAW CAKES — Teisennau Berffro

Abberffraw cakes are made from a Victoria sandwich cake mixture and sprinkled with sugar after baking. In Aberffraw, scallop shells were used as cake tins.

1 oz (25 g) sugar
2 oz (50 g) butter
3 oz (75 g) flour
1 oz (25 g) sugar for sprinkling on top of the cakes

Cream the butter and sugar together.

Add the flour and mix well by hand.

The mixture should be soft and easy to work.

Roll out fairly thinly on a floured surface.

Cut into rounds and bake in a moderate oven for about 15 minutes.

Sprinkle with sugar after baking.

Oven: 350°/190°C   Gas Mark 5

DOUGHNUTS

An old recipe for making doughnuts without yeast, that is quick and easy.

½ lb (225 g) plain flour
2 teaspoons baking powder
A pinch of salt
2 oz (50 g) butter
2 oz (50 g) sugar
1 egg beaten
A little milk
½ lb (225 g) lard for cooking

Sift the flour, baking powder and the salt.

Rub in the butter and add the sugar.

Add the beaten egg and sufficient milk to make a nice dough.

Roll out on a floured surface and cut into rounds.

Put into boiling fat and cook until light brown.

SYRUP LOAF — Torth Sirop

12 oz (350 g) self-raising flour
A pinch of salt
2 oz (50 g) sugar
2 oz (50 g) raisins
The grated rind of an orange
¼ pint (150 ml/⅔ cup) syrup
1 egg
¼ pint (150 ml/⅔ cup) milk

Mix together the flour, salt, sugar, raisins, orange rind and the syrup.

Beat the egg and add to the mixture with the milk.

Mix thoroughly and put into greased bread tin.

Bake in a moderate oven for about one hour.

Serve thinly sliced and buttered.

Oven: 350°F/180°C   Gas Mark 4

WELSH GINGERBREAD —
Teisen Sinsir Gymreig

Gingerbread is made for bonfire night in Wales. It was also traditionally made for fairs. Originally the gingerbread did not have ginger in it.

Use golden syrup if you prefer a lighter coloured gingerbread and treacle for a darker gingerbread.

½ lb (225 g) flour
1 tablespoon demerara sugar
3 oz (75 g) butter
¼ lb (100 g) treacle or golden syrup
2 teaspoons ground ginger
1 egg beaten
3 tablespoons milk
½ teaspoon bicarbonate of soda

Melt the sugar, butter and treacle in a small pan over a gentle heat.

Remove from the heat.

Mix the ground ginger with the flour and blend with the treacle mixture.

Add a well beaten egg.

Warm the milk and dissolve the soda in it.

Add to the gingerbread mixture and beat until well mixed.

Grease a shallow baking tin.

Pour in the mixture.

Brush the top with milk and bake in a moderate oven for 40 minutes or until a skewer comes out clean from the gingerbread.

Allow to cool a little and cut into squares.

Oven: 375°F/190°C   Gas Mark 5

BAKESTONE BREAD — Bara Planc

For many generations the 'planc' has been an integral part of the Welsh kitchen and many are still used today. It is generally known as 'planc' meaning an iron plate for baking bread but has other regional names such as ffroesen, pancogen and pancosen. The bakestone was traditionally a quick way of making bread, pancakes and cakes - a heavy black frying pan may be used instead.

A planc is more commonly known as a griddle in England.

1 lb (450 g) plain flour
A pinch of salt
½ oz (15 g) yeast
1 teaspoon sugar
½ pint (300 ml/1¼ cups) warm milk
½ oz (15 g) lard or other fat

Sift the flour with the salt.

Cream together the sugar and the yeast adding a little of the warm liquid.

Leave for a few minutes to froth.

Rub the fat into the flour.

Add the yeast and the remaining milk and mix to a smooth dough.

Knead well.

Leave to rise until double its size.

Roll out ½ lb (225 g) of the bread on a floured surface.

Shape it into a flat 6 inch (15 cm) round about 1 inch (2.5 cm) thick and flatten the top with a rolling pin.

Cook slowly on a well greased bakestone or heavy frying pan.

Do not allow the bakestone to become too hot or the bread will burn on the outside.

Cook both sides until golden brown.

A traditional way to serve the bread is to cut the loaf in half, butter it well and then put it back together.

Butter the top and eat it hot.

BARA BECA

8 fl oz (250 ml/1 cup) water
6 oz (175 g) caster sugar
6 oz (175 g) sultanas or dried fruit
1 egg, beaten
8 oz (225 g) self-raising flour
½ teaspoon mixed spice
A pinch of salt

Put the water, sugar, dried fruit and margarine in a saucepan.

Cook over a gentle heat, simmering for five minutes.

Allow to cool a little.

Add the beaten egg, flour, spice and salt.

Mix well to form a soft dropping mixture.

Pour into a greased tin and bake in a moderate oven for about an hour.

Oven: 350°F/180°C   Gas Mark 4

CURRANT OR SPECKLED BREAD —
Bara Brith

Bara Brith is the National Bun loaf of Wales and means speckled bread. It is a delicious currant bread that is more traditionally made with yeast, but methods without yeast are also popular and just as good.

Bara Brith is common to all Celtic countries and there are many different recipes within Wales itself.

1 lb (450 g) plain flour
4 oz (100 g) lard or butter
4 oz (100 g) brown sugar (not demerara)
6 oz (175 g) raisins
6 oz (175 g) currants
3 oz (75 g) candied peel
½ teaspoon mixed spice
A pinch of salt
½ pint (300 ml/1¼ cups) warmed milk
1 oz (25 g) yeast
1 egg, beaten

Mix the yeast with the warm milk and leave to stand in a warm place for 10-15 minutes until frothy.

Rub the fat into the flour until the mixture resembles fine breadcrumbs.

Stir in the sugar, raisins, currants, peel, spice and salt.

Make a well in the centre and add the yeast and the well-beaten eggs.

Mix into a soft dough and cover and leave in a warm place to rise to twice its size.

Turn on to a floured surface and knead well.

Put the mixture into a 2 lb (900 g) greased bread tin and cover and leave for a further 20-30 minutes.

Bake in a moderate oven for 1-1½ hours or until golden brown.

Bake in a moderate oven for 1-1½ hours or until golden brown.

Allow to cool before serving, sliced and spread with butter.

Oven: 400°F/200°C   Gas Mark 6

BARA BRITH (Without Yeast)

1 lb (450 g) self-raising flour
8 oz (225 g) lard
6 oz (175 g) sugar
8 oz (225 g) mixed dried fruit
2 eggs, beaten
A little milk

Rub the fat into the flour until it resembles fine bread-crumbs.

Mix in the sugar and dried fruit.

Add the beaten eggs and enough milk to make a soft dropping mixture.

Bake in a moderate oven for about 1½-2 hours or until golden brown.

Test with a skewer. If the skewer comes out clean the bara brith is cooked.

Oven: 350°F/180°C   Gas Mark 4

PLANK PASTRY — Teisen Planc

An excellent way of using up left-over pastry.

½ lb (225 g) sweet shortcrust pastry
4 oz (100 g) jam
Caster sugar

Roll out the pastry to about ¼ inch (5 mm) thick and cut into two rounds about 8 inch (20 cm) in diameter.

Spread one round with the jam leaving an edge around the pastry.

Place the other round on top to make a lid.

Moisten the edges and seal.

Bake slowly on greased bakestone, griddle, or heavy frying pan, and turn during cooking.

When golden brown on either side, sprinkle with sugar and serve.

WELSH CAKES — Pice ar y Maen

Pice ar y maen, meaning cakes on the stone are traditional little cakes, and are a speciality of South Wales, though still popular throughout the country. Mainly cooked on the bakestone or griddle they can also be baked in a heavy pan. Cherries were sometimes used instead of currants and sometimes spices were added. This is the 19th century recipe of a farmer's wife.

1 lb (450 g) plain flour
1 teaspoon baking powder
2 oz (50 g) sugar
4 oz (100 g) currants
1 egg beaten
Cream
2 oz (50 g) butter
2 oz (50 g) sugar for dusting

Mix together the flour, baking powder, sugar and the fruit.

Stir in the egg and the cream to make a soft paste.

Roll out on a floured surface.

Cut into 2 inch (5 cm) rounds about ¼ inch (5 mm) thick.

Bake on a greased bakestone, griddle or heavy frying pan for a few minutes each side or until nicely browned.

Serve hot with a knob of butter and a sprinkling of sugar on the top of each cake.

The Welsh Cakes may be allowed to cool and will keep for a few days in an airtight container, but they are best eaten as fresh as possible.

OATCAKES — Bara Ceirch

Makes about 24 oatcakes

Bara meaning bread illustrates the importance of oatcakes as part of the staple diet in past centuries. Oatcakes were mainly baked on the bakestone but they were also made in the oven. A Crafell, a special wooden instrument, was used for putting them in and taking them out of the oven.

Welsh oatcakes were traditionally made as large as possible, 8-10 inches (20-25 cm) across. They must be made with oatmeal that is not coarse and then left to harden after baking. They can be eaten alone or with a meal, but always with a glass of buttermilk.

This recipe combines flour with oatmeal making the cakes less likely to break. It requires great skill to make a thin oatcake without a crack. Traditionally, however, they are made without flour.

14 oz (400 g) medium oatmeal
2 oz (50 g) flour
¼ teaspoon of salt
1 teaspoon of sugar
6 tablespoons of dripping or other fat
Hot water for mixing

Warm the mixing bowl and add the dry ingredients, mixing well.

Rub in the fat and knead to a soft dough adding a little water if necessary.

Roll the dough out quickly on a floured board.

Cut into 3 inch (7.5 cm) rounds.

Place on a greased baking tray and bake in a hot oven for 15-20 minutes or bake on a moderately hot bakestone, griddle, or thick frying pan, allowing 7-8 minutes per side.

Serve buttered.

Oven: 425°F/220°C   Gas Mark 7

SLAPAN

Slapan must be eaten hot. It can be cut in half and buttered.

1 lb (450 g) flour
8 oz (225 g) butter
8 oz (225 g) sugar
4 oz (100 g) currants
4 eggs
Lard for frying

Rub the butter with the flour until it resembles fine breadcrumbs.

Beat the eggs well and mix them with the flour.

Add the currants and the sugar mixing well.

Cook spoonfuls of the mixture on a hot greased bakestone, griddle, or frying pan.

Fry both sides until browned and eat hot.

PIKELETS — Bara Pyglyd

Pikelets are small yeast pancakes, similar to crumpets or muffins although they are thicker. Pikelets as they are known in England, are believed to come from the Welsh name 'Pyglyd' meaning pitchy bread. Pikelets would be cooked on a bakestone, griddle, or hotplate. As they cook holes should appear, which are characteristic and hold the melted butter when they are served.

1 lb (450 g) flour
1 oz (25 g) yeast
1 teaspoon sugar
1 pint (600 ml/2½ cups) warm milk
1 egg beaten
A pinch of salt

Mix the yeast with the sugar.

Add the warmed milk.

Sieve the flour with the salt.

Make a well in the centre and add the milk gradually.

Mix in the beaten egg and beat the batter well until smooth.

Cover the bowl and leave the batter in a warm place to rise for at least an hour.

Drop the batter in spoonfuls on to a hot and lightly greased bakestone or frying pan.

Cook both sides until golden brown.

Serve hot with butter and jam, honey or syrup.

98

WELSH PANCAKES — Crempog
Serves 6

Crempog is a favourite for tea, but also makes an excellent pudding or savoury. The traditional way was to make large pancakes, spread them with butter, pile one on top of the other, cut into quarters and serve them hot. Sweeter versions are also popular such as crempog with sprinkled sugar, golden syrup, honey or jam: in Anglesey, it was often blackberry jelly. Savoury fillings such as seafood, onions and herbs are also good.

Crempog would have been cooked on a bakestone or griddle. A heavy greased frying pan may be used instead.

8 oz (225 g) plain flour
½ level teaspoon of bicarbonate of soda
A pinch of salt
1 egg
½ pint (300 ml/1¼ cups) buttermilk or milk to mix
1 oz (25 g) lard for frying
2 oz (50 g) butter

Sift the flour salt and the bicarbonate of soda together.

Make a well in the centre and add the egg and a little milk.

Beat well with a wooden spoon and gradually add the remaining milk.

Continue beating for a few minutes to make a smooth batter.

Grease the frying pan, girdle or hot plate with the lard.

When the fat is hot drop four tablespoons of the mixture into the pan ensuring the batter covers the bottom.

Cook for two minutes or until golden brown.

Turn and cook for one minute on the other side.

Keep the pancakes warm in the oven and continue to make the rest of the pancakes in the same way.

Serve hot spread with butter.

CAERPHILLY SCONES — Sgonau Caerffili

Makes about 10 scones

Caerphilly was originally a Welsh cheese although now it is also produced in England. Today, traditional farmhouse cheeses such as Caerphilly, cheddar and goats cheeses are still made by some dairies in Wales.

8 oz (225 g) flour
2 teaspoons baking powder
A pinch of salt
1 oz (25 g) butter
3 oz (75 g) Caerphilly cheese, grated
A little pepper to taste
Milk for mixing
1 egg, beaten, for glazing

Sift the flour with the baking powder and the salt.

Rub the butter into the flour until the mixture resembles fine breadcrumbs.

Add the grated cheese and pepper to taste.

Add enough milk to make a soft, firm dough.

Roll out on a floured board to about ½ inch (1 cm) thick.

Cut 3 inch (7.5 cm) rounds and place on a greased baking tray.

Brush the top of each scone with a little egg and bake in a hot oven for about 10-15 minutes.

Serve hot with butter.

Oven: 425°F/220°C   Gas Mark 7

FRUIT GIRDLE SCONES — Teisen Gri

8 oz (225 g) flour
1 teaspoon cream of tartar
½ teaspoon of bicarbonate of soda
1 oz (25 g) butter
2 oz (50 g) seedless raisins
1 oz (25 g) caster sugar
1 egg beaten
¼ pint (150 ml/⅔ cup) milk

Sieve together the flour, cream of tartar and the bicarbonate of soda.

Rub in the butter.

Add the fruit and mix in the sugar.

Add the well beaten eggs and enough milk to make a soft dough.

Roll out on a floured surface to about ½ inch (1 cm) thick.

Cut into rounds.

Cook the scones on a hot greased girdle (griddle) or in a heavy frying pan.

If preferred the scones may be baked in a hot oven for about 15 minutes.

MARROW PICKLE

4 lbs (1.75 kg) marrow
Salt to cover
4 onions
4 shallots
¼ oz (7 g) ground ginger
2 oz (50 g) mustard
½ oz (15 g) turmeric
½ lb (225 g) sugar
4 chillies
8 cloves
3 pints (1.75 litres/6 cups) vinegar

Peel and remove the seeds from the marrow.

Cut it into 1 inch (2.5 cm) squares.

Place in a bowl, cover with salt and leave overnight.

Rinse and strain.

Peel and chop the onions and shallots.

Tie the chillies and cloves in a muslin bag.

Put it in a preserving pan with the marrow, ginger, mustard, turmeric, sugar and vinegar.

Bring to the boil and then simmer rapidly until the vegetables are tender, and the mixture is thick.

Remove the muslin bag.

Pot into warmed dry jars and cover.

There is no need to store the preserve before using.

VEGETABLE MARROW AND LEMON CURD

Makes about 3 lbs (1.5 kg)

2 lbs (900 g) when prepared of vegetable marrow
Salt
2 lbs (900 g) preserving sugar
2 large lemons
4 oz (100 g) butter

Peel the marrow, remove the seeds and cut it into quarters.

Put 2 lbs (900 g) of the slices into a saucepan of boiling salted water.

Simmer until tender.

Strain, and leave the marrow in a sieve to dry completely.

Beat the marrow to a smooth pulp.

Put in a preserving pan with the sugar, the grated rind and strained juice of the lemons, and the butter.

Stir over a gentle heat until the sugar is dissolved and the butter melted.

Boil until the curd is thick and smooth.

Pot and cover as for jam.

MARROW AND GINGER JAM

Makes about 6 lbs
(2.7 kg)

4 lbs (1.75 kg) when prepared, of vegetable marrow
3 lemons
4 lbs (1.75 kg) preserving sugar
2 oz (50 g) root ginger

Peel the marrow, remove the seeds and cut it into 1 inch (2.5 cm) cubes.

Cut the rinds of the lemons into thin strips and squeeze the juice.

Put the marrow, sugar, lemon rind and juice into a preserving pan and allow to stand overnight.

Bruise the ginger with a weight to release the flavour, and tie it in a piece of muslin.

Add the ginger to the other ingredients in the pan, and boil all together, stirring occasionally and skimming if required until setting point is reached and the marrow looks transparent.

To test for setting put a little jam on a cold saucer, and if it wrinkles when pushed with the little finger, it is ready.

Remove the muslin bag of ginger.

Pot in hot dry jars and cover with purchased jam covers.

104

BRAMBLE JELLY

When making bramble jelly. lemon juice can be used instead of apples.
Allow the juice of 1 lemon to each 1 lb (450 g) of blackberries and add
with the sugar.

3 lbs (1.5 kg) blackberries
1½ lbs (675 g) cooking apples
8 fl oz (250 ml/1 cup) water
1 lb (450 g) preserving sugar to every 1 pint (600 ml/2
  cups) of juice yielded

Prepare the blackberries.

Quarter and core the apples, but do not peel.

Place the fruit in a preserving pan with the water and
simmer until quite soft.

Put the fruit pulp mixture into a jelly bag, and leave preferably overnight until all the juice has dripped through.

Do not squeeze the bag to hasten the process, or to yield
more, as the finished jelly will not be clear.

Measure the juice obtained, and stir in 1 lb (450 g) preserving sugar for every 1 pint (600 ml/2 cups).

Heat gently in the preserving pan, stirring frequently,
until setting point is reached.

To test for setting put a little syrup on a cold saucer and
leave to cool. If the jelly wrinkles when pushed with the
little finger, it is set.

Ladle into warmed jars.

Cover and store as jam.

LEMON CHEESE — Caws Lemwn

Makes 1 lb (450 g)

¼ lb (100 g) butter
1 lb (100 g) granulated or loaf sugar
Juice of 3 lemons
6 yolks of eggs
Grated rind of 2 lemons

Put the butter, sugar and lemon juice into a saucepan over a low heat to melt.

Beat the yolks of eggs well and add to the mixture with the lemon rind.

Stir until the mixture thickens, taking care not to allow the mixture to boil.

Allow to cool.

Put the cheese into pots and cover as for jam.

Carrot Marmalade

From Eliza Sloughter's recipe book dated 1771.

'Take any quantity of carrots when in perfection and put them into a closed vessel with as much water as will prevent them from burning when in your oven. When cold put them through a seive to a pound of carrot pulp, put one pound of white sugar, lemon juice sufficient to give it an acid flavour but do not put it in til quite cold if put in jars it will keep two years.'

ORANGE MARMALADE — Marmalêd

12 Seville oranges
4 sweet oranges
2 lemons
3 pints (1.7 litres/6 cups) water to every 1 lb (450 g) fruit yielded
1 lb (450 g) preserving sugar to every 1 lb (450 g) of pulp yielded

Slice all of the fruit very finely.

Remove and retain the pips.

To every pound of sliced fruit add 3 pints (1.75 litres/6 cups) of water.

Let the mixture stand overnight to soften the peel.

Pour a little boiling water over the pips and leave this also to stand overnight.

Strain.

Add the pip liquid to the fruit.

Simmer the mixture in a preserving pan for about one hour until the peel is tender, and the liquid reduced.

To every pound of pulp stir in 1 lb (450 g) of preserving sugar.

Boil the mixture again until setting point is reached.

To test for setting point put a little of the marmalade on a cold saucer; if it wrinkles when pushed gently with a finger, it is done.

Stir well, and put into clean dry jars.

Cover with purchased jam covers.

TANGY PLUM SAUCE

This sauce is excellent with traditional fried breakfast, cold meat and pies.

2 lbs (900 g) Victoria plums
1 large onion
6 oz (175 g) dried fruit (not candied peel)
3-4 oz (75-100 g) brown sugar
1 teaspoon of mixed spice
A pinch of ginger
½ pint (300 ml/1 ¼ cups) brown vinegar
Black pepper and a dash of salt

Stone the plums.

Peel and chop the onion.

Put all the ingredients in a thick bottomed pan.

Cover and simmer for an hour or until the mixture is thick and 'mushy'.

Press the sauce through a sieve or liquidize.

Bottle and leave for 6 weeks before using.

LAVER SAUCE   Serves 4

A sauce that is especially good served as an accompaniment to roast lamb. If serving with shellfish such as lobster, use double cream instead of gravy.

8 oz (225 g) prepared laver
1 oz (25 g) butter
1 pint (600 ml/2 ½ cups) thick gravy made from the pan juices used to roast the lamb
Juice from 1 Seville orange
Salt and pepper

Put the prepared laver into a saucepan with the butter, gravy and orange juice.

Season with salt and pepper to taste.

Heat, stirring, until hot.

ONION SAUCE — Saws Nionod

4 medium onions
2 oz (50 g) butter or margarine
2 oz (50 g) flour
18 fl oz (550 ml) milk
2 fl oz (3 tablespoons/¼ cup) double cream
Salt and pepper

Peel the onions and cook them gently in a little salted water until tender.

Drain and chop them finely.

Melt the butter in a saucepan, and stir in the flour.

Cook for 2 or 3 minutes, stirring.

Gradually stir in the milk.

Bring to the boil and then cook gently, still stirring until the sauce thickens.

Season with salt and pepper to taste.

Add the chopped onions.

If a smooth sauce is preferred, liquidize or rub the mixture through a sieve.

Swirl in the cream just before serving.

Reheat, but do not allow to boil again.

GINGER BEER — Diod Sinsir

This very old recipe will make a very good ginger beer.

'To ten gallons of water put eight pounds of loaf sugar, four ounces of ginger sliced, boil it an hour take off the scum as it rises, then empty it into a tub let it stand till it is cold, afterwards put it into a barrel, put the peel and juice of ten lemons, half spoonful of yeast at the top, stop it up close, the lemons must be sliced very thin and the juice strained, in a fortnight it will be fine to bottle and in another ready to drink, it is intended to add a bottle of brandy.'

For smaller quantities try:

1 gallon = 8 pints (4.5 litres) water
1¼ lb (575 g) loaf sugar
½ oz (15 g) of ginger
1 lemon
½ oz (15 g) yeast
Brandy (optional)

To Make Beef Tea

From Eliza Sloughter's recipe book dated 1771.

'Take a peice of Beef that has not been salted and cut it in as thin slices as possible and put a pound of it to quart of Water and set it on a quick fire and from the time it boils scim it continuously til there arises not the least scum. it must boil for twenty minutes as quick as possible let it stand for two hours then pour it of and season it with a blade of Mace and a little Salt.'

MEAD — Medd Hen Ffasiwn (Metheglin)

8 pints (4.5 litres) water
2 lbs (900 g) honey
**1 pint (600 ml/2½ cups) of white wine for every gallon (8
pints/4.5 litres) of liquid**
1 oz (25 g) yeast
The peel of 2 lemons
2 bruised whole nutmegs

Bring the water and the honey to the boil.

Remove any scum from the surface and simmer gently
for about an hour.

Pour into an earthenware pot and leave to cool to blood
temperature.

Add the yeast and leave it to work.

When it has stopped 'hissing' add the white wine and the
lemon peel.

Hang two bruised nutmegs in the liquid and leave it for
about a week.

Strain and bottle.

Do not cork until the liquid stops bubbling.

Keep the mead for at least 6 months before drinking.
It will improve with age.

LEMON AND ORANGE CORDIAL

A refreshing summer drink.

3 oranges
3 lemons
2 lbs (900 g) sugar
1 ½ pints (900 ml/3¾ cups) boiling water
½ pint (300 ml/1¼ cups) cold water
1 oz (25 g) citric acid

Thinly peel the skin from the fruit and squeeze the juice.

Put the peel, juice and sugar into a basin and pour over the boiling water.

Stir well until the sugar melts.

Cover the basin and leave it to stand overnight.

Dissolve the citric acid in the cold water.

Stir it into the ingredients.

Strain the cordial into a jug, and bottle.

Dilute with water before drinking.

The cordial will keep well, stored in a cold place or refrigerator, for up to three months.

TREACLE TOFFEE — Cyflaith

Makes about ¼ lb (100 g) toffee

Toffee was part of the New Year's Eve festivities in the 19th century. It was a custom for all the family to help make the sweets and of course to eat them when celebrating the New Year.

4 oz (100 g) butter
6 oz (175 g) demerara sugar
2 tablespoons treacle
A drop of milk
A drop of vinegar

Melt the butter, sugar and treacle in a pan.

Bring the ingredients to the boil and add a drop of milk milk and then stir in a drop of vinegar.

Continue cooking for a further 10 minutes or until the toffee is set.

Test for setting by putting a few drops of the toffee mixture into cold water. When it is set it will harden at once.

Pour the mixture into a greased tin and mark into squares.

Leave in a cool place to set.

When it is cold, break the toffee into pieces.

LLYMRU

Llymru is the Welsh version of flummery, an oatmeal cereal. It can be eaten with milk, treacle or honey. A coarser version, known as Sucan in South Wales, is made from shelled oats, using soaked husks and leavings.

2 lb (900 g) oatmeal
Buttermilk
Water

Mix the oatmeal with enough buttermilk and water to make a liquid consistency.

Leave it for 2 nights.

Rinse and strain off the liquid through a sieve.

Let it stand and then pour off the surface water.

Bring to boil and simmer for 40 minutes, stirring all the time.

Cure for a Tight Chest

Mrs. Hannah Meurig-Jones recalls a visit by Aunt Frances to her home in Ammaford: "When my husband, Meurig, was in bed with a tight chest cold, I suggested many cures but to no avail. Aunt Frances arrived, looked at Meurig and asked for lard, mustard and brown paper. She mixed the lard and mustard together and spread it on the brown paper. I gleefully watched her placing the 'plaster' on my husband's chest, because he didn't have the courage to say 'no' to her.

The following day, Meurig removed the 'plaster' with the comment "My chest is like a ruddy sunset, and it's a wonder that I have a hair left!"

Although this is not a recommended recipe - his chest was cured.

Acknowledgements

Grateful thanks are extended to the many people of Wales who have contributed towards this collection of recipes, especially:

Maureen Hughes of Mold, Clwyd, for Treacle Toffee and Orange Lamb Delight.

Mrs. M. Jones of Denbigh, Clwyd, for Shearing Cake, Plate Cake or Teisen Lap and Lemon and Orange Cordial.

Timothy Jones of Ponthirwaun, Cardigan, for Doughnuts, Tenby Cake, Soda Cake, Lemon Cheese, Orange Marmalade, Marrow Pickle, Galantine of Beef, and Curried Eggs from his Aunt's recipe book.

Anne Evans of Portmadog, Gwynedd, for Rhubarb Cake, and Bara Brith without yeast from her Grandmother's recipe book.

Mrs. M. Owen of Bridgend, Glamorgan, for Welsh Rarebit, Bara Brith, Bakestone Fruit Tart, Savoury Faggots, and Leekie Pie.

Joanne Duggan of Penarth, South Glamorgan, for Welsh Cheese Cakes, Bakestone Bread, and Bacon Broth or Cawl.

Mai Evans of Goodwick, Dyfed, for Potato Cake.

Anne Thomas of Burry Port, Dyfed, for Trollies; and her Great Grandmother's Welsh Cakes.

Miss E. Bynner-Griffiths of Beaumaris, Anglesey, for Cat Crispies, Caraway Biscuits, Casserole of Mutton Chops with Vegetables, Welsh Pudding, Welsh Gingerbread, Fruit Girdle Scones, and Crempog.

Dorothy Hughes of Abergavenny, Gwent, for Fish Cakes, Lemon Pie, Leek Pasty, Marrow and Ginger Jam, and Vegetable Marrow and Lemon Curd from her late Sister's recipe collection.

Hannah Meurig-Jones from Annaford for Cure for a Tight Chest.

Mrs. J. Steventon of Trelogan, Clwyd, for Welsh Shoulder of Lamb with Puff Pastry, Winter Hasty Leeks, Leek and Bacon Duff, Jacket Potatoes with Leek and Bacon Filling, Roast Leg of Lamb with Scallions and Apricots, Tangy Plum Sauce, Bacon Ribs with Broad Bean Sauce and Game Pie - many from her Grandmother, a professional cook's recipe book.

Mrs. M. Davies of Abercynon, Glamorgan, for Corned Beef and Potato Pie.

Mrs. M. Edwards of Rhyl, Clwyd, for Rabbit Stew.

Joyce Hadyn Jones, Chairman, of the Committee of the Newton (Swansea) Ladies Guild of the Missions to Seamen, for Welsh Lamb Hot Pot, Stuffed Roast Goose, and the Miser's Feast.

Mr. S. J. Davis of Cardiff for Bara Beca from St. Mark's Church recipe book.

Mary Hancock of Prestatyn, Clwyd, for Bacon Ribs and Cabbage.

Richard Treble, Chef of The Seiont Manor Hotel, Caernarfon, Gwynedd, for Fillet of Arctic Char, and Boned Saddle of Lamb stuffed with Baby Leeks, with Rosemary Sauce.

John Sealey, Head Chef of The Beaufort Hotel, Tintern, Gwent, for Port and Stilton Paté with Hazel Nuts, and Baked Trout with Oatcakes and Honey.

David Collett, Chef of The George III Hotel, Penmaenpool, Dolgellau, Gwynedd, for Poached Salmon Steak with Prawn, Mushroom and Cucumber Sauce.

Marion and Steve Williams, owners of The White Horse Inn, Llandeilo, Dyfed, for Cockle and Laverbread Pancakes and Lemon and Elderflower Sorbet.

The National Library of Wales, Aberystwyth, for kind permission to include Potato Pudding, Beef Tea, Carrot Marmalade, Beef with Cabbage Sauce and For a Hung Goose from Eliza Sloughter's recipe book dated 1771; Ginger Beer, and Almond Cheesecake from the Glansevern Collection of handwritten recipes; Lady Betty Warburton's Biscuit Cake from Lady Elizabeth Warburton's recipe book; A Very Good Common Cake from Mary Burchinshaw's recipe collection; To make Artichoak Pie and A Tart of Rice from Rebekah Jones her book 1740, which is among the collection of Mrs. P. M. Williams' of Welshpool, Powys.

Special thanks for information from:

Ann Chettoe of Wrexham, Clwyd; Mrs. M. Davies of Bangor, Gwynedd; Glenys Evans of Swansea, Mr W. Morgan of Brigend, Mid Glamorgan, and Mike and Sandie Hughes of Aberfforest Marine, Fishguard, Dyfed.

For baking the Bara Brith and Welsh Cakes on the front cover, grateful thanks are given to Mrs. Jane Jones of Bwrdd Croeso Cymru.

THE COUNTRY RECIPE SERIES

Available now @ £1.95 each

Cambridgeshire
Cornwall
Cumberland & Westmorland
Derbyshire
Devon
Dorset
Gloucestershire
Hampshire
Kent
Lancashire
Leicestershire
Norfolk
Northumberland & Durham
Oxfordshire
Somerset
Suffolk
Sussex
Warwickshire
Wiltshire
Yorkshire

All these books are available at your local bookshop or newsagent, or can be ordered direct from the publisher. Just tick the titles you require and fill in the form below. Prices and availability subject to change without notice.

Ravette Books Limited, 3 Glenside Estate, Star Road, Partridge Green Horsham, West Sussex RH13 8RA.

Please send a cheque or postal order, and allow the following for postage and packing. UK 25p for one book and 10p for each additional book ordered.

Name ....

Address ....

....

....